# making
# WOOD
# SIGNS

## Patrick Spielman

Sterling Publishing Co., Inc.   New York

Metric Conversion Chart

| | | |
|---|---|---|
| ⅛ inch = 3.18 millimetres | ⅝ inch = 15.88 millimetres | 1½ inch = 38.10 millimetres |
| ¼ inch = 6.35 millimetres | ¾ inch = 19.05 millimetres | 2 inches = 50.80 millimetres |
| ⅜ inch = 9.53 millimetres | ⅞ inch = 22.23 millimetres | 1 foot = 30.48 centimetres |
| ½ inch = 12.70 millimetres | 1 inch = 25.40 millimetres | 1 yard = 0.9144 metre |
| | 10 millimetres = 1 centimetre | |

**Library of Congress Cataloging in Publication Data**
Spielman, Patrick E.
  Making wood signs.
  Includes index.
  1. Woodwork.  2. Signs and sign-boards.  I. Title.
TT200.S6      674'.88      80-54342
ISBN 0-8069-5434-5      AACR2
ISBN 0-8069-8984-X (pbk.)
ISBN 0-8069-5435-3 (lib. bdg.)

Copyright © 1981 by Patrick Spielman
Published by Sterling Publishing Co., Inc.
387 Park Avenue South, New York, N.Y. 10016
Distributed in Canada by Sterling Publishing
℅ Canadian Manda Group, P.O. Box 920, Station U
Toronto, Ontario, Canada M8Z 5P9
Distributed in Great Britain and Europe by Cassell PLC
Artillery House, Artillery Row, London SW1P 1RT, England
Distributed in Australia by Capricorn Ltd.
P.O. Box 665, Lane Cove, NSW 2066
*Manufactured in the United States of America*

# Table of Contents

# Acknowledgments

With more than just loving support and understanding, my wife, Patricia, has been actively and devotedly involved in all aspects of our family business from the beginning. Her exceptional and varied talents, along with her overall dedication to excellence, have been the very springboard that makes this book possible. Artistic and creative energies always pour forth. They are exclusively hers, and measurably the greater part of all of our joint efforts.

The work of some highly skilled sign craftsmen helped to expand the scope of this book and was the source for many of its illustrations. Many thanks to the late Bill Beckstrom for his indirect influence, to Douglas Williams and Bill Schnute for their outstanding carved signs, to Arwed Barnowsky and his crew for their nifty post work, and the following individuals and organizations whose skills are valued and illustrated: Pudge DeGraff, Lynn Charney, Brian Daubner, Bob Spielman, Charles Kinsey, Collins-La Crosse Sign Corp., Sign Classics, Inc., Jason Morgan, The Old Oak Shop, Lis Kukla, Don Zinngrabe (Calligrapher), and some excellent but unknown craftsmen in Florida — photographs of their signs appear herein. A special thanks to Tom Swormstedt, Associate Editor of *Signs of the Times* magazine, for his supportive contributions and cooperation.

The following companies have provided auxiliary materials and illustrations: Adjustable Clamp Company, ALC Company, Inc., Bendix Mouldings, Inc., Black and Decker Co., Buck Brothers, Dowel-It-Company, Greenlee Tools, The Kimball Co., Laskowski Enterprises, Marlin Industries, Millers Falls Co., P. K. Lindsay Co., Rockwell Power Tools, Sears-Roebuck Co., and Stanley Tools. The California Redwood Association provided some excellent illustrations and technical data.

We do appreciate immensely all of our customers whose signs were photographed for this book — and thanks especially to Dorothy and Pete Kortes of the English Inn for their timely confidence in our abilities.

# Introduction

Signs abound all around us. They direct, locate, restrict, inform, identify, motivate, and sometimes aggravate our daily lives. Signs give us good and bad messages of all sorts. Flickering neon, lighted plastic, and rusting metal signs obscure and cheapen commercial areas across the country. Conversely, wood signs blend in (Illus. 1) with all environments and offer a desirable change of pace.

The continuing popularity of authentic, well-crafted wood signs is very real, and the reasons are manyfold. Perhaps the major reason is that wood itself has a quality of uniqueness and individuality that stands eloquently alone—enduring and "honest." This very quality has led many plastic and metal sign companies to imitate the appearance of wood with artificial graining and texturing. This is not design integrity and we all know it. Authentic wood signs do not give a deceptive impression. Whatever the message of an authentic wood sign, we subconsciously assume that it is said sincerely and honestly. Remember, a sign is your "front door." It gives others their very first impression of your home, business, farm, or community.

Wood signs have many other advantages over their offensive plastic and neon counterparts. Wood signs truly blend in with natural environments (Illus. 2),

*Illus. 1 (left). A park preserving the giant redwoods. Note how the unobtrusive sign blends in with the surroundings.*

*Illus. 2 (below). Another example of how nicely wood street signs harmonize with the natural surroundings.*

*Illus. 3. Wood signs endure and actually become more beautiful with time. (Designed and crafted by Pudge DeGraff.)*

trees, foliage, shrubbery, stone, or water. Beautiful country landscapes and architecture can be least disturbed by unobtrusive, well-executed wood signs. Yet, they delicately and effectively attract the eye because they are each unique. Wood signs maintain their desired natural appearance for a long time, much longer than other kinds of signs which eventually fade, blister, crack, rust, or literally fall apart. When assembled and finished properly, wood signs become more beautiful with age. Regardless of what most people think, wood signs best endure the turbulent natural elements of moisture, sun's rays, snow, sleet, ice, and so on. They also best resist vandalism. As wood signs get older, they impart an impression of endurance, long establishment, and permanence. See Illustration 3.

Wood signs can be easily fabricated to take advantage of three-dimensional design. Letters, numbers, and decorations can be (1) cut into the surface, (2) raised from the backing, or (3) a combination of both (Illus. 4).

This book is heavily illustrated with sample signs in many shapes, styles, and sizes. These will be very helpful to you whether you are a novice or an accomplished producer of wood signs.

Becoming skilled at wood sign work is easy. One can start small and work up to larger or more involved signs, with each new one offering a different challenge. There are essentially two distinct areas of proficiency that one should continually strive to improve upon and eventually master. These are (1) design and (2) execution of basic woodworking skills. Making quality wood signs requires an intimate marriage of graphic design and technical woodworking. Many books are available devoted to each subject. This book, for the most part, will not deal with or repeat this type of information. However, in the following pages you will be guided, step-by-step, through each area of wood sign work.

*Illus. 4 (above). Effective combination of cutout letters (attached) with engraved (cut-in) letters and design logo makes a very attractive sign. (Designer and fabricator unknown.)*

*Illus. 5 (right). A sign simply executed with individual letters sawn out and attached to produce a raised letter effect.*

Each new sign will improve your expertise and before long you will have people knocking on your door requesting your skills.

At this point you may want to turn sign-making into a business enterprise. You can start small with a minimum of equipment—with just the bare necessities of a knife and chisel you can learn to carve eloquent wood signs (Illus. 3). With a coping saw or a portable saber saw you can cut out letters of any size and style (Illus. 5). This book offers little advice on sign business management. However, it must be pointed out that a good business potential does exist. Why? Everyone loves wood and almost everyone needs some sort of signage. Think about it for a moment! Developers of residential areas and home owners want entrance signs, name signs, house numbers, and street signs (Illus. 6). Business and professional people want impressive, distinctive signage. City, county, and other public agencies need signs to identify and direct people to roads, parks, recreational areas, and public buildings. Professionals, who make small routed name signs freehand or by machine, when set up in shopping centers, fairs, and tourist areas, can gross $500 daily. The potential is out there if you want it. It only takes time and practice to build a reputation for quality wood signs.

This book will show you how to make a good start in producing different kinds of popular wood signs. One chapter deals with basic hand-carved signs (Illus. 7).

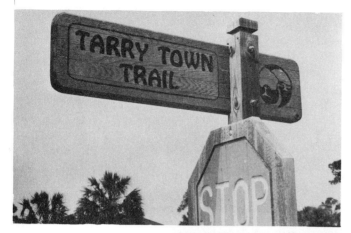

*Illus. 6. This example of wooden street signage in a Florida development is both unique and attractive. (Designer and fabricator unknown.)*

*Illus. 7. Hand-carved wood signs require a minimum of tools, but more effort than other kinds of wood signs. (Refer to chapter 5.)*

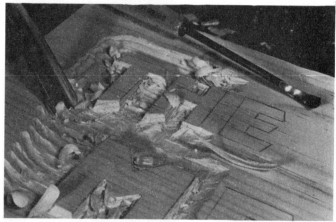

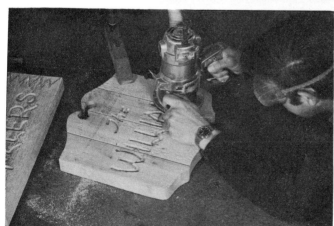

*Illus. 8. Freehand routing produces small signs quickly, as shown by this single-stroke work. (Refer to chapter 6.)*

*Illus. 9 (left). Another example of an incised routed sign —just one among endless possibilities. (Refer to chapter 6.)*

*Illus. 10 (above). These examples of sandblasted work illustrate the wide range of this sign-making technique. (Refer to chapter 10.)*

Another deals with cutout or sawn letters. Several chapters are devoted to routed signs (Illus. 8 and 9), as these are currently the most popular and offer the greatest speed and variety of manufacture. Also included is a chapter covering sandblasting (Illus. 10), the newest area of wood sign work. Throughout the book are tips, shortcuts, and advice offered on subjects of design, material selection, tools and machines, finishing, and related project ideas.

Unless otherwise indicated, the signs illustrated as examples in this book have been fabricated by the author. In the back of the book you will find an extensive list of company names and addresses where you can order catalogs, supplies, and equipment that may not be available locally.

# 1 Woods for Sign-Making

The selection of wood materials for sign-making should be based upon the following requirements:

(1) Service (interior or exterior)—exposure to humidity, sun's rays, weather, etc.

(2) Desired appearance (overall design effect)—smooth, slick, modern, or rough and rustic.

(3) Workability—sawn-out letter work does not require the easy cutting properties that hand and router carving does.

(4) Freedom from defects—will cracks, knots, or warpage detract from the sign's appearance or interfere with cutting operations?

(5) Cost—do not skimp. A better grade, although more expensive, will eliminate much aggravation.

(6) Availability—can you always get it quickly and easily (locally) or must it be shipped to you?

**Woods for Interior Signs** have only one important criterion. They must be properly dried. Almost any species or kind of wood material can be used as long as it gives you the desired appearance and is dried to a moisture content appropriate for interior use. All fine furniture hardwoods can be used for indoor signs. Kiln-dried mahogany, walnut, butternut, cherry, and so on, are ideal for hand-carved or router-carved signs. Softwoods such as pine, redwood, basswood, and cedar are very desirable for all kinds of work.

*Illus. 11. A supply of 2-inch white cedar for exterior signs is piled and stickered for air drying.*

**Woods for Exterior Signs** do not need to be kiln dried, but they must not be green either. A moisture content of 12 to 15 percent is a very satisfactory range for most parts of the country. This level can be achieved by proper air drying of fresh-cut boards or lumber (Illus. 11). Redwood is one of the best overall choices, but its major disadvantage lies in its high cost. Western red cedar, northern white cedar, and cypress are more economical. They have similar positive properties in their resistance to the deteriorating effects of decay and weathering. However, redwood is generally regarded to be far superior in its easy working properties. Any type of wood can be used for exterior signs if it is kept high and dry. However, most signs are usually exposed to the sun's rays and moisture. During weathering, some species of wood may degrade more rapidly than others. Brief descriptions of various woods and their suitability for exterior signs follow:

**Basswood** is soft and lightweight. The heartwood is pale, yellowish brown with occasional darker streaks. Its sapwood is creamy-white or pale brown. Basswood does not, as a rule, have attractive graining and it is usually painted or stained with opaque finishes. It has a fine, even texture and straight grain which makes it easy to work, especially for hand-carved signs. Basswood does not have exceptional weathering qualities so it must be carefully finished. Basswood grows in the eastern half of the United States. Most of it comes from the lake, mid-Atlantic, and central states.

**Cypress** grows commercially in the southern states. The color varies widely. Its sapwood is narrow and nearly white. The heartwood ranges from light yellowish brown to dark brownish red, brown or chocolate. It is moderately hard and one of our most decay-resistant woods, making it especially useful for sign posts. As a rule, it is not the easiest wood to carve by hand or with the router.

**Douglas Fir** essentially comes from the northwestern coastal and Rocky Mountain states. It has rapid growth, as often characterized by its graining and spacing of growth rings. The difference in hardness between spring and summer growth often makes it difficult to router-carve cleanly and smoothly. It does not weather well, with a high tendency to check and distort in hot and dry environments. Douglas fir is fairly economical. Rough-sawn Douglas fir (lumber and plywood) does make attractive signs, but it must be properly finished for exterior use.

**Pine.** There are many kinds of pine. White pine, ponderosa pine, and sugar pine rank high in dimensional stability with little shrinkage or distortion. Clear, knot-free pieces are ideal for hand and router carving, with sugar pine being the best. Lower grades can be used for rustic signs. Southern yellow pines

*Illus. 12 (left). Some common sign-making materials include rough-sawn planks (cedar), smooth 1- and 2-inch boards (redwood), and resin-coated-paper-overlaid plywood. Illus. 13 (right). Redwood has a uniform texture and other excellent qualities for hand-carving, routing (shown), and sandblasting.*

are inexpensive but do not have the good overall qualities for carving and routing of the other pines. The pines will weather well if properly finished and kept away from soil and excessive moisture.

**Spruce** is very similar in appearance and color to pine, but the varieties from the southern states have more difficult working properties. It is essentially a construction material, as is Douglas fir. It is economical and readily available at most lumber yards and building centers. Eastern spruce is light in color with little difference between its heartwood and sapwood. It is easily dried, light-weight, easily worked, and has moderate shrinkage. Its appearance makes it suitable for interior sandblasted signs.

**Cedar** is of two major types: white and red. The cedars are among the best overall choices for exterior sign work. Their best qualities include economy, high resistance to decay, ease of workability, and good weathering. The cedars are generally straight grained and have uniform texture. They sandblast well and are easily carved by hand or router. They are lightweight, moderately soft, and easily dried.

The red cedars grow in the eastern forests and some limited areas of the south Atlantic and gulf coastal plains. A similar species, western red cedar, grows primarily in the Pacific northwest. The heartwood of red cedar is reddish brown to dull brown and the sapwood is nearly white.

White cedar grows in the Atlantic states and eastern part of the United

States. The greatest sources are probably in Maine and in the Great Lake states. The heartwood of white cedar is very light brown and the sapwood is nearly white. It is lightweight and shrinks very little in drying. It is easily worked, highly resistant to decay, and holds finishes exceptionally well. White cedar can be router-cut cleanly and some of it sandblasts well, depending on how it is cut from the tree.

**Redwood** (Illus. 12 and 13) grows principally in California, but it is available nationwide. The sapwood is nearly white. It is very easy to work because of its straight and uniform grain. Redwood shrinks or swells very little and it is highly resistant to decay. In short, redwood is a good choice for any kind of wooden sign work. It is the easiest of any wood to sandblast. Its only disadvantage is its comparatively high cost for clear and select grades. However, because of its overall superior qualities, it is usually worth the extra expense. Sometimes the costs can be offset by purchasing a lower grade, such as "construction." Often, small clear pieces can be cut out between knots and glued together again to make large clear pieces. Redwood and cypress are the only two woods that are naturally resistant to termites.

**Pressure-Treated Wood** is now available to the home craftsman at lumberyards and building centers. In this special wood, preservatives are forced deeply into cellular fibres with large vacuum-pressure treating systems. The preservatives prevent wood-destroying organisms from getting to their food source, thereby protecting the wood from decay and rot. The treating process results in wood with a soft green color that needs no further finishing. However, pressure-treated wood is stainable or it can be painted any color. Pressure-treated wood is available in several wood species with southern pine being very widely used. It is generally heavier than comparable untreated wood as it is saturated with preservatives. Pressure-treated wood is highly recommended for posts in contact with soil and moisture.

It is possible to give regular non-treated posts a brush-on or dip treatment of creosote (preservative) yourself but the long-term protection is not nearly as great as with pressure-treated wood. The service life of dry, treated pine in contact with the soil is two to five years. A brush-on application will add one to three more years. A dip treatment gives 1/10 to 1/8 inch penetration and will give an added service life of five to ten years. Pressure treatment lasts a lifetime.

**Selecting and Buying Lumber** for wood signs, as for any worthwhile woodworking project, should be done carefully. Check to see what kinds of materials are available locally. As mentioned before, signs for outdoor use do not need to be made from kiln-dried wood, but the wood should be dried to the point where it is in equilibrium with the moisture in the surrounding atmosphere. In northern

*Illus. 14. Giving a smooth board a rough-sawn texture. Here the surface is pulled lightly backwards along a band saw blade.*

Wisconsin, for example, fresh-cut lumber is available for direct purchase from small sawmills. It must be stacked outside and allowed to dry from six months to a year before use (Illus. 11). Signboards can be 1 or 2 inches thick, with the latter preferred for two-sided and larger signs.

In northern Wisconsin, signs with rough-sawn surfaces are seemingly more popular than those made of smoothly surfaced stock. Rough-sawn stock can be purchased directly from sawmills and rough-sawn western cedar and redwood are often available at lumberyards. It is possible to give a smooth board a rough-sawn textured surface yourself. Simply pull it backwards obliquely along the blade of the band saw as shown in Illustration 14. It can also be done on the table saw. However, in this case you feed the stock as usual along the rip fence. Use an old blade with a tooth set out a greater distance than the rest. This tooth will "chew up" the surface, giving it a rough-sawn appearance.

It is suggested that rough-sawn boards be touch-sanded lightly (Illus. 15). This light sanding highlights the texture and removes protruding slivers and fibres that make layout and routing difficult.

Obviously your design should be worked out before you select and prepare your stock. Thus, you can position patterns to avoid knots or other defects before cutting the sign blank to final size and shape.

Remember that when purchasing smooth-surfaced boards from lumberyards, they are finished to less than their nominal (name) or rough-sawn size. For example, you know that when you buy a "two-by-four," it actually measures 1½ inches by 3½ inches. A 6-inch board is 5½ inches wide, an 8-inch board is 7¼ inches, a 10-inch board is 9¼ inches and a 12-inch plank is actually 11¼ inches wide. It is a good idea to check construction sites, and with local carpenters and builders, to see if suitable scraps may be available for small signs or practice pieces.

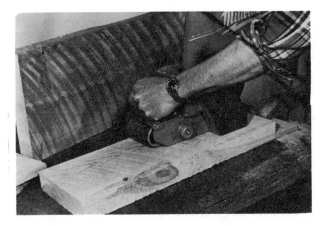
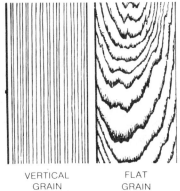

VERTICAL
GRAIN

FLAT
GRAIN

*Illus. 15 (left). Rough-sawn boards are lightly touch-sanded to highlight the texture and, at the same time, remove problem slivers or protruding fibres. Illus. 16 (right). The difference between vertical and flat-sawn wood. Boards with vertical grain are more dimensionally stable and tend to warp much less than boards with flat grain.*

**Lumber Grain Patterns** (Illus. 16). Boards and planks are cut from the log in different ways—usually with "vertical" or "flat" grained faces. You will find that in most species of wood the boards with flat grain tend to cup and warp a lot more readily than boards with vertical grain. Some species may be more difficult to router-cut or sandblast on vertical grain than flat grain. This is especially true with Douglas fir and some cedars.

It is also important to remember that vertical-grain boards are more dimensionally stable than flat-cut boards of the same wood. In other words, vertical-grained boards do not shrink or swell in size across their width as much as flat-grained boards do. This is an important consideration if the signboards are to be encased or circled by a wooden frame. Allowance should be made for wood expansion when putting frames around signs of solid wood.

*Illus. 17. This routed sign with the hand-hewn effect is easy to do.*

*Illus. 18 (above). Surfaces of big timber posts can be worked with the adze to produce a hewn appearance.*

*Illus. 19 (top right). Make cross-grain cuts randomly with a hatchet.*

*Illus. 20 (center right). Using an inshave to "chew-up" the edge. Make some cuts against, as well as with, the grain.*

*Illus. 21 (bottom right). The surface is worked in the same manner. Hatchets, chisels, adzes, and so on, can also be used, but the inshave produces the best routing surface.*

*Illus. 22 (above). This slab from a saw mill would have little value as lumber but makes a good rustic sign.*

*Illus. 23 (right). A slab cut diagonally from a tree creates a very natural look.*

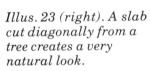

**Hand-Hewn** signs (Illus. 17) and posts (Illus. 18) are very popular, as these represent an era of the long, long past. Hand-hewn planks can be effectively simulated by texturing the surfaces with various edge tools as shown in Illustrations 19–21.

**Rustic Slab Signs** of all sorts can be made with a little imagination. Slabs from sawmill edgings, or slabs you simply cut yourself with a chain saw, make effective and unusual signs, as shown in Illustrations 22 and 23. Slabs can also be treated with polyethylene glycol to keep the bark on (refer to the book *Working Green Wood With PEG*, also published by Sterling). Small slabs of this type (Illus. 24) are also becoming more easily accessible at art and craft shops. They are also available by mail order. See the source listing in the Appendix.

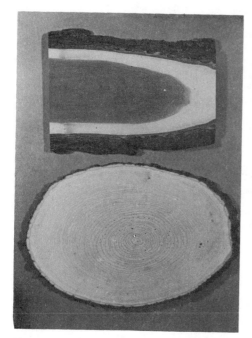 

*Illus. 24 (left). Slabs cut in different directions give different shapes. Illus. 25 (right). This large routed sign with irregular profile shape is best made of plywood. Note the rough-sawn texture. It was spray-painted black and then touch-sanded to highlight the saw marks.*

**Plywoods and Other Sheet Materials** are often required for certain, usually larger signs. Exterior plywoods with rough-sawn surfaces are available, particularly in fir, cedar, and redwood. Smooth, exterior fir plywood has little esthetic value in sign work. It is primarily used as a backing that is either not visible in the structure or completely painted to opaque its wild grain. Even when carefully painted, the grains often eventually "telegraph" through the finish, which is objectionable in the eyes of some people. A new sheet material especially designed for smooth, painted surfaces is available. This is a plywood with a resin-coated-paper-overlaid surface (Illus. 12). This material is ideal for making inexpensive cutout letters that will be painted and attached to another sign backing. Plywoods are obviously not suited to hand carving and sandblasting. However, they do deserve consideration for router-carved signs (Illus. 25). The glue lines will dull ordinary high-speed steel router bits quickly. Carbide bits will not dull nearly as quickly, so they should be used when routing plywoods and other hardwoods.

# 2　Designing Wood Signs

A properly executed sign is one that is expertly crafted from a good design. Design is at first thought to demand some very rare, magical, creative, and artistic talents. Obviously, possessing these qualities would be helpful. However, if you are not a "natural" or you are untrained in graphic artistry, don't be discouraged. This chapter will assist you to the point where you can create well-defined, artistic wood signs quickly and easily. See Illustrations 26–28.

Give careful attention and critical study to all of the signs you see daily. Soon you will notice that some have that "something special" while others do not. Try to distinguish just what it is that makes one sign more appealing than another. Is it the choice of letter style, appropriate size and spacing, color, arrangement and combination of individual elements, or what? Study the signs illustrated throughout the pages of this book. Many are of rustic motif, yet appear to be

*Illus. 26 (top left). Small name signs are good "starters." Illus. 27 (bottom left). Large, bold, block letters are easy to read. Illus. 28 (right). A very basic sign. Note how the rounded corners and pegs help to make the sign interesting.*

*Illus. 29 (above). Wood in a contemporary design. (Designed and fabricated by Collins —LaCrosse Sign Corp.)*

*Illus. 30 (right). A "woodsy" look is emphasized in this modern sandblasted sign. (Designed and fabricated by Sign Classics, Inc.)*

carefully planned and executed. Others are designed to fit into more modern and contemporary surroundings (Illus. 29 and 30).

Problems may arise if modern signs have crude or rustic lettering. Be careful when using modern, smooth material for rustic-shaped sign plaques or backings. Be sure that the materials, the overall design, and the selected finish all complement each other. It's crude, for example, to put bright fluorescent colors or paints on wood signs—especially those of a rustic, "pure wood" motif. If that is to be done, one may as well settle for plastic or neon signs that are capable of drawing that kind of attention.

Use your own imagination along with selected desirable features from signs that appeal to you. With an awareness of all kinds of signs you will soon establish your own priorities and individual standards of good design and taste. You will become capable and confident when judging sign design qualities.

Your first and primary concern may be originality. Do not worry about this. Copy and use the alphabets and plaque designs provided in the Appendix and throughout this book. Each sign will be your creation because it will have its own wording, as well as individual symbols, logos, or appropriate decorations to complement the lettering or overall effect.

The first technical consideration is to establish the desirable size (height) of the individual letters. Be conscious of the fact that signs are located at various distances from the viewer. Letters that may appear to be very large sitting on your workbench diminish rapidly in size as they are positioned progressively farther away. Consequently, determine the maximum required distance from which the sign must be easily read. Certain styles of letters are more legible than others. Bold, fat, simple block letters are the easiest to read—especially if the viewer is traveling by in a motor vehicle. The traveling speed of the viewer, his/her visual acuity, color contrast, and the presence of distracting surroundings are some of the variables that make strict rules for letter sizes difficult to establish. However, the following chart may be helpful as a guide to determine the optimum letter sizes for people with 20/20 vision.

| Distance (in feet) | Letter Sizes (height in inches) |
|---|---|
| 100 | 1¾ to 2 |
| 200 | 3½ |
| 400 | 7 |
| 600 | 10½ |
| 800 | 14 |
| 1,000 | 17½ |
| 1,300 | 22 to 25 |

Once the preferred letter height is determined, and assuming total space is no problem, enlarge the sign letters to this size. Be sure to arrange or allow for appropriate spacing between letters (and words) so the "art" is easily readable. One key point is to eliminate unnecessary wording. Discourage the inclusion of too much information. In the case of a small residential sign, for example, people will often want both parents' first names, the family name, each child's name, the house number, and, "Oh yes, put the cat's name angled in the corner so it isn't confused with being one of the children."

The alphabets in the Appendix and other chapters are only a few of the hundreds of typefaces available to the wood-sign-maker. These few were selected for their suitability to cutting and they are generally easy to read—not too ornate ("cute") and not crude or amateurish in style. Determine whether the words are to be all capitals, lower case, or a combination of both. Larger letters require more space between them and more space between words and lines. Give some thought to borders around the sign (Illus. 31). Allow appropriate space for borders.

Any of the letters can be enlarged by the graph-square or the same grid system commonly used to enlarge patterns for woodworking projects. Make your patterns on paper so they can be revised as necessary and saved for possible reuse.

Full-size, enlarged letter patterns in various typefaces and sizes can also be purchased (see the source listing in the Appendix). They are available in the form of full-size printed plans or as die-cut letters (templates) in plastic, wood, and cardboard (Illus. 32).

*Illus. 31. Some border ideas and corner designs.*

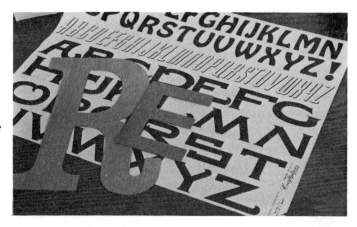

*Illus. 32. Full-size alphabets are available in print from companies that provide full-size paper patterns for woodworking projects. Also shown are full-size pre-cut plywood templates which can be homemade or purchased pre-machined.*

**Letter Spacing** is an important design consideration. Letters should not be crowded too closely together or have unequal gaps. The letter *A*, for example, fits more closely next to *T* than *E* or *M*. Once the word is composed and laid out full size, step back the maximum distance and view it critically. Have others look at it and get their opinions. Does the sign have character? Is it clean and crisp? Is there continuity in style? Does it convey satisfactorily the intended theme or feeling? A good, well-spaced, properly aligned, and consistently styled letter arrangement will work for you. Make your layout on paper first, so changes can be made as necessary until you achieve your standard of perfection. (Note: Be sure, at this point, as well as immediately before carving, to have the sign's originator check it for accuracy.)

**Arranging the Words.** Determine which geometric profile shape is most appropriate for the sign. Here we may be allowed a choice of: (1) rectangular-horizontal, (2) square or round, or (3) rectangular-vertical (Illus. 33). Most all signs will fit into one of the above categories. The selection of the most suitable

*Illus. 33. Arrange the words to complement the different geometric shapes.*

*Illus. 34 (top left). Size can be used to give emphasis to important words. Illus. 35 (bottom left). Variety was the challenge from these three identical boards. Note how each sign is interesting in itself through the use of different letter sizes. Illus. 36 (right). A vertical layout. Note the clarity achieved with the different styles and sizes of letters.*

overall sign profile from the above three may be dictated by various require-ments: (1) the width and height of the area in which the sign will eventually be hung or placed, and (2) the type of signpost that may already exist. Study Illustrations 34–42. Often you may have to "play" with trial-and-error layouts,

*Illus. 37. Individual, pre-cut, full-size letter patterns, such as these of cardboard, make "trial-and-error" layout easy.*

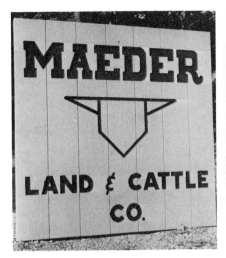

*Illus. 38 (left). A perfectly square sign with logo and wording centered. Illus. 39 (right). Another (basically) square sign, but here the layout is not symmetrical.*

*Illus. 40 (top left). Extending the vertical "legs" on some letters adds an element of height to the layout without increasing width. Illus. 41 (bottom left). A curved layout can be an interesting arrangement that reduces length as well. Illus. 42 (right). The size and shape of the sign determine the layout.*

using scaled pencil sketches on graph paper to match the optimum letter size and the desired arrangement and order of words. The object is to fit everything satisfactorily onto a sign blank of the desired overall shape. When confronting this sort of problem, be sure to give consideration to the overall shape of the total sign before finalizing the height of the letters. Very often the letters will have to be reduced or enlarged slightly more than expected to fill up excess blank space or avoid crowding.

Professional sign-makers and painters confront and solve these problems without difficulty—often by pure instinct tempered with much experience. Other professionals (with less experience) opt to purchase the service of professional sign pattern companies. These services provide to the sign-maker custom full-size paper pattern layouts of complete signs with any letter style (typeface), all fit properly and professionally into any space or overall sign shape. These services utilize sophisticated computer graphics systems. A digitizer converts the pattern shapes into digital data and eventually a "plotter" transforms the data into a full-sized drawing, providing a properly spaced sign pattern. (See the Appendix for sources of full-size pattern services and other design supplies.)

Amateurs and beginners wanting to make their enlarged layouts faster and easier will find the use of enlarging projectors more suitable than the graph-square method for their design work. The two basic kinds of projectors are *opaque* and *overhead*.

**Opaque Projectors** create an enlarged image of any non-transparent object. Printed pages, photographs, and drawings in black and white or color can be

*Illus. 43 (left). An overhead projector can be used to enlarge images in a lighted room.*

*Illus. 44 (below). Pressure-sensitive lettering can be selected from catalogs. Shown is 180-point type (1¾ inches high)—about the largest available.*

26

*Illus. 45. To apply dry transfer letters for the preparation of original art work: first, rub with a dull pencil, ballpoint pen or similar blunt instrument (left); then, lift the sheet carefully (right).*

enlarged easily. Opaque projectors range in price from very inexpensive to very expensive. They all work best in a darkened room.

**Overhead Projectors** (Illus. 43) project bright, enlarged images in a lighted room. They will enlarge to any size from a 10-inch-square transparency (transparent acetate, clear plastic, or glass) which lies flat on the face or stage of the projector. The overhead projector is, as a rule, less expensive than a good opaque projector. The image is always clearly reproduced. Overhead projectors are more convenient, more portable, and more versatile.

While overhead projectors are fairly expensive items to purchase, they can often be rented or borrowed. They are available through camera or audio-visual equipment supply stores. (Also, see the listing in the Appendix.) Schools widely use overhead projectors.

**Preparing Art for Projection.** Enlargement begins by using the same lettering aids technical artists use, known as dry-transfer or rub-on letters. These consist of pre-printed lettering on pressure-sensitive sheets as shown in Illustration 44. They are easy to use. Simply transfer the letters to another surface by burnishing (rubbing) over the letter on the carrier sheet as shown in Illustration 45. Wide selections of typefaces, borders, designs, and symbols are available. Dry-transfer supplies are relatively inexpensive and can be purchased at office supply stores, artist-craft shops, or directly by mail order (see the listing in the Appendix).

The dry-transfer letters are transferred to a sheet of clear plastic film or even directly onto a piece of window glass. This layout is then placed on the projector table and an enlargement of any size can be made by moving the projector toward or away from the projecting surface (a wall will do). Once the desired size

*Illus. 46 (left). Here, individual letters are traced from an enlarged projected alphabet. Illus. 47 (right). Complete alphabets can be transferred to transparency sheets and subsequently enlarged to any size desired.*

is achieved, the enlarged image is traced (Illus. 46). It can be traced onto paper (for a permanent copy) or it can be traced directly onto the wood sign blank. We usually make a paper copy and then refine the traced lines and the work and space arrangement before transferring the design to the wood. The paper patterns are retained and the copies make useful sales tools.

Sooner or later someone will want you to reproduce a specific design from a printed business letterhead, sales brochure, or newspaper ad. Designs of this type can be enlarged in one of two ways: (1) draw squares over it and enlarge it freehand by the graph-square or grid method, or (2) have a transparency made of it which is subsequently enlarged on the overhead projector. A transparency of any printed art can be made for you by anyone who owns a thermo-copier transparency-making machine. Most schools have this equipment, as do major business offices and some public libraries. It only takes a few seconds to have a transparency made. We use the 3-M Thermo-Fax® copier-transparency maker. Use their transparency film 8½ × 10½ inches type 588 which produces a black image on a clear background (Illus. 47–49).

Once you have gone through the processes of using press-on letters, overhead projection enlargement, and making transparencies, you will see how very simple copying, enlarging, and designing really is. This experience will be your most valuable design asset. Any conceivable design or pattern can be copied and enlarged for your own creative sign work (Illus. 50). Soon you will be clipping magazine ads, leafing through children's coloring books, and digging into similar resources. Before long you will have a file of designs which can be combined with various alphabets to make truly superb custom-designed signs.

Once you get into sign-making, commercial jobs will begin to come your way. Often the client will supply his own design, or will be financially able to hire a

*Illus. 48 (above). A transparency film can be made from a newspaper advertisement.*

*Illus. 49 (right). The enlarged ad, projected from transparency film by an overhead projector, can then be traced.*

commercial graphic artist to design his sign. Some will approach you and provide you with the full-size layout. Then all you have to do is transfer it to the wood and carve, rout, or blast the design, in or out as preferred.

**Transferring the Pattern to the Wood** is a simple task, as shown in Illustrations 51 and 52. Illustration 51 shows a paper sign pattern being traced and transferred to the wood with carbon paper. Illustration 52 shows the use of a "pounce wheel." Before removing patterns, be sure that all lines have been transferred. On rough-sawn surfaces we use carbon paper *and* a pounce wheel

*Illus. 50. The finished sign in wood. This one was made by sandblasting.*

*Illus. 51 (left). Transferring the enlarged pattern to the wood with carbon paper.
Illus. 52 (right). Using a pounce wheel makes the transferral of large patterns
quick and easy.*

*Illus. 53. The layout
can be chalked in to
make it easier to see
during routing.*

because it is difficult to see clearly all the tooth markings of the pounce wheel on
these surfaces. When transferring patterns to smoothly surfaced wood with a
pounce wheel, the carbon paper can be eliminated.

After the letter patterns are outlined on the wood, silhouette them with chalk
(Illus. 53) or soft-tip markers. This is especially helpful when doing freehand
router carving so you know which side of the line to cut on and which areas need
to be removed or left uncut.

Review various graphic arts and design books. Any and all bits and pieces of
information will help you design your first signs. Later, with more of your own
experiences to assist you, each new sign will become easier and easier to design.
It will also be done with much less time, effort, and worry about overall quality
because you will know it is there and it is good.

# 3   Basic Tools and Machines

You will need the obvious array of small household hand tools, including tape or bench rules, straightedges, squares, hammers, screwdrivers, and so on. Here, let's take a brief look at some of the additional tools and machines that are basic to most wood sign fabricators. This chapter will omit the usual "how-to" operating and safety instructions because this information is probably redundant for most of you and is very adequately presented in many other books devoted to wood crafts. (Check at your local library.) However, particular instructions that apply specifically to the craft of making wood signs will be presented later in other chapters, such as those devoted to carving, sawing, routing, and sandblasting. If you do not own or have access to the tools or power equipment, check with the rental services that may be found in most cities. If you are just beginning you may also consider jobbing out some of the work to local professionals, such as carpenters, cabinetmakers, or other woodworkers.

**Saws.** Any good handsaw or portable circular saw, suitable for straight-line ripping and crosscutting, is a must item for sizing your material. The table saw (Illus. 54) makes both crosscuts and ripping cuts quickly and accurately. For making cuts that are irregular or curved, you can use a simple coping saw (Illus.

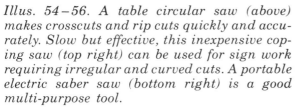

*Illus. 54–56. A table circular saw (above) makes crosscuts and rip cuts quickly and accurately. Slow but effective, this inexpensive coping saw (top right) can be used for sign work requiring irregular and curved cuts. A portable electric saber saw (bottom right) is a good multi-purpose tool.*

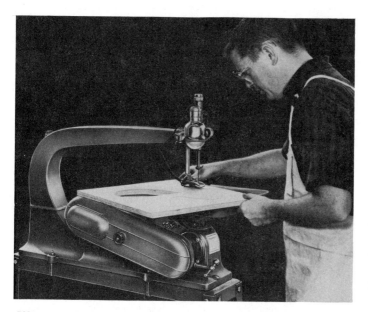

*Illus. 57 (left). The jigsaw is ideal for making cutout letters and similar inside or outside curved cuts. Illus. 58 (right). The band saw makes easy work of both straight and irregular cuts in thin or thick materials.*

55), a portable electric saber saw (Illus. 56), a jigsaw (Illus. 57), or a band saw (Illus. 58).

**Planing Tools** are often necessary for smoothing the surfaces and edges of sawn boards. Planes are used to prepare boards for gluing into wider or thicker sizes. Unless planing tools are available, it is necessary to always purchase material that is already planed to your specified finished size. Various kinds of hand planes (Illus. 59) are available. Portable power planes are also available, but they are expensive and have little advantage over well-sharpened, properly adjusted hand planes. Serious woodworkers like to use the jointer (Illus. 60) for trueing the edges and surfaces of boards. A thickness planer (Illus. 61) is a luxury piece of equipment unless you are a full-time professional woodworker or sign-maker. This machine reduces boards to uniform parallel thickness.

**Shaping Tools and Routers** are required if a sign is to be given an interesting shape or formed edge, with an overall professional look to it. A lot of sign work can be done by a skilled craftsman using simple, ordinary chisels and gouges (Illus. 62 and 63). Various wood files or rasps are helpful in making hand-carved signs. A simple jackknife or utility knife (Illus. 64) is very useful in the hands of a skilled "sign mechanic."

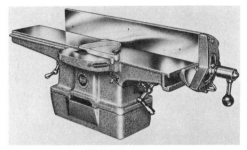

*Illus. 59 (above). Planing the edge of a board with a jack plane in preparation for gluing.*

*Illus. 60 (top right). A small jointer can do big planing jobs.*

*Illus. 61 (bottom right). A thickness planer smooths and reduces rough boards to true parallel thicknesses.*

The portable electric router (Illus. 65) is a whole shop in itself because of the wide range of bits and attachments that are available. Routers come in many sizes, styles, and with various standard or optional features. Some makers of routed signs prefer a very small, lightweight, high-rpm tool for working red-wood and for edge-forming work. Others, like myself, prefer a heavy, high-powered unit for making deeper and wider cuts in tougher woods. Features that are worth considering when purchasing a router for sign work include: weight, rpm, horsepower, type of on-off switch, lighted work area, vacuum attachment, collet size (bit capacity), and the availability of parts and repair service.

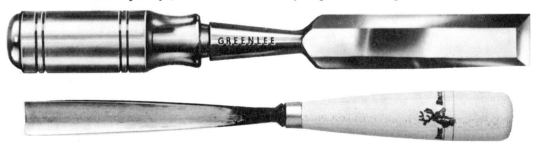

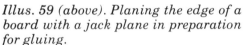

*Illus. 62 and 63. Chisels (top) and gouges (bottom) are inexpensive yet necessary tools for **making hand**-carved signs.*

33

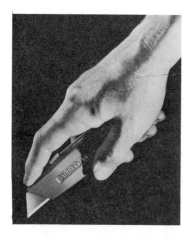

*Illus. 64 (left). This utility knife with sharpenable or replaceable blades is very useful.*

*Illus. 65 (right). A router is one of the most important tools for the serious sign-maker. Many different features are available to satisfy individual needs and preferences.*

Having a router that will carry bits larger than the usual ¼-inch shank diameter affords the craftsman the opportunity to purchase and use bits available for large production, industrial routing machines.

**Router Bits** (Illus. 66). The old saying, "You get what you pay for," is especially true here. Inexpensive bits are good for a few jobs. They can be resharpened when dull, but the problem is that they dull quickly. Good quality, high-speed steel bits hold up very well when routing softwoods such as redwood. However, the cedars (particularly the white cedars) dull even the best high-speed

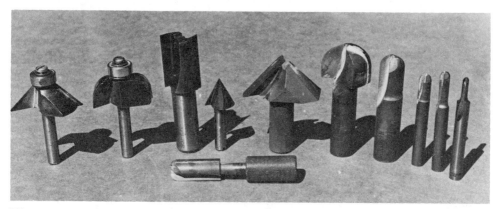

*Illus. 66. A selection of router bits that are widely used in sign-making. Left to right are ball-bearing-piloted edge-forming bits, straight and "V" cutting bits, and round-nose bits of various sizes. Most are carbide-tipped and the smaller ones are solid carbide. The bit in the foreground is a specially ground "bottoming" bit which makes a wide cut with curved inside corners and a flat bottom.*

*Illus. 67 (top). Expansive bit is adjustable for large holes of any size. Illus. 68 (bottom). Spade bits like this, used to make holes up to 1 inch in diameter, are available to fit ¼-inch electric drills.*

steel bits rather quickly. Good carbide bits are probably more economical and they will give you less grief and frustration in the long run. Note, there is good carbide and cheap carbide as well. When shopping for carbide-tipped bits, look for thick carbide. Some bits are tipped with carbide that is too thin, and after one or two sharpenings the carbide becomes dangerously thin and the bit must be thrown away. Remember that carbide requires special grinding wheels. It is strongly recommended that all of your bits be sent out to professional resharpening services. Bits must not only have proper clearance angles, but they must be properly balanced as well; otherwise their ultra-high-speed vibrations are both dangerous and difficult to handle skillfully.

The **Drilling or Boring** of holes is often necessary for one job or another. This class of work can be done using the old bit and brace, the portable electric drill, or the drill press machine. An adjustable expansive bit (Illus. 67) is useful for making large holes of any size. If you own a small portable electric hand drill (with only a ¼-inch chuck), consider buying a set of spade bits (Illus. 68) which will allow you to drill holes up to 1 inch in diameter with your small drill.

**Dowel Jigs** are available in several different styles. A good one is often a tremendous help to the serious sign-maker. It is especially helpful when gluing boards edge to edge to make large sign blanks. Dowels in this case are used more for the purpose of aligning the pieces during gluing rather than imparting additional joint strength. If glued properly, edge-to-edge joints are stronger than the wood itself.

**Clamps** are needed when gluing and assembling larger signs. Bar clamps (Illus. 69) (or clamp head fittings for pipe) are necessary when gluing boards

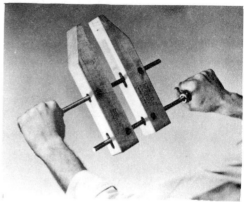

*Illus. 69 (left). Boards **glued edge to edge with bar** clamps. Illus. 70 (right). Handscrew clamps have many uses.*

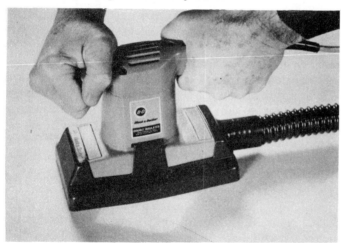

*Illus. 71. A pad sander can be used for finish work. Note the dust-collecting attachment.*

together edge to edge. Handscrew clamps (Illus. 70) or "C" clamps are used to hold work steady for carving and routing by clamping it to benches. They are also used to apply pressure when gluing pieces of wood face to face to make a thicker piece.

**Sanders.** Here again individual preferences will vary. Pad or vibrating sanders (Illus. 71) are nice for fine finishing work. Belt sanders are more powerful and cut faster.

# 4　Cutout Letters

There really isn't anything especially difficult about making cutout letters (Illus. 72). Any fairly imaginative and reasonably proficient woodworker can enlarge and saw out individual letters, compose them into words, attach them to some sort of panel backing, and presto!—you have a fabulous, dimensionally interesting sign. This chapter will provide some ideas for such signs and offer a few tips to make this class of sign work even easier.

**Background Sign Panels.** Using plywood panels for sign backing makes the job especially easy. Very large wood signs can be made stronger, faster, and more economically with plywood backings than with any of the other wood sign systems described in this book. Several kinds of exterior-grade sheet plywoods are available with interestingly textured surfaces. Check with your building materials supplier and you will probably find plain, rough-sawn fir, cedar, and redwood in textured, grooved (Illus. 73), reverse board and batten, and other suitable designs. They all make excellent backgrounds for cutout raised letters. The

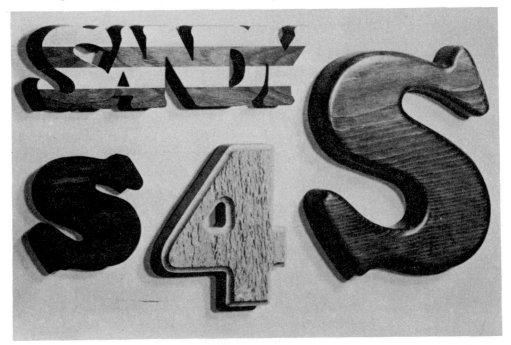

*Illus. 72. Different materials and finishes give different effects. Counterclockwise from top left: letters run together in edge-laminated woods; veneer-faced plywood; solid rough-sawn cedar; solid finished pine.*

*Illus. 73 (left). The grooved plywood backing shown here allows for quick assembly of the sign backing. (Designed and fabricated by Charles Kinsey.) Illus. 74 (right). Vertical cedar boards were nailed to horizontal two-by-four cleats to make the background for this interesting sign.*

perimeter edges of the plywood backing panels can be left alone, or they can be covered with solid wood frames and/or set into grooves in the supporting post structures.

Solid lumber (boards) nailed (with corrosion-resistant nails) to two-by-four cross cleats, **with** the grain running vertically (Illus. 74), horizontally, or ob-

*Illus. 75. Solid, weathered wood, diagonally planked, makes an attractive background for the painted cutout plywood lettering of this sign, seen along a Florida highway. (Designer and fabricator unknown.)*

liquely at 45 degrees (Illus. 75), and left unframed, make interesting sign backings.

**Plywood Cutout Letters** (Illus. 75) have several advantages over letters cut from solid wood. They do not crack or warp, and they can be made in very large sizes (height and width) without gluing. For letters and decorations that will be painted with opaque, pigmented finishes, any exterior sheet materials can be used. There is available a resin-coated-kraft-paper-overlaid plywood which is ideal for smooth, uniform surfaces that are to be painted. One serious disadvantage of plywood is that it seldom is available in sizes thicker than ¾ inch. Consequently, to achieve anything thicker two or more pieces must be glued together face to face. If good glues are used and the letters well-sealed and finished, they will endure the exterior elements as long or longer than plastic-formed letters.

**Making Cutout Letters of Solid Wood** requires some precautions—especially if the letters are to be exposed to the weather. Most letters look better if they are cut from the wood with the grain running vertically on the face of the letter. Select letter styles that are "fatter" with few thin or narrow areas. Regardless, most letters will have areas of "short grain." An example of short grain is shown in Illustration 76. These areas are the weakest parts of the letters, and cracks or separations might develop during drastic changes in humidity and temperature. Plywood letters obviously do not have this problem because the veneer plies are assembled with alternating grain directions. However, the cut edges of plywood may be unattractive to some people, particularly if transparent stains are selected for finishing. Conversely, thicker solid wood letters have a

*Illus. 76 (left). This beautiful thick letter of solid wood may crack at the area of "short grain" pointed out here. Illus. 77 (right). Thin plywood glued to the back of a solid wood letter prevents cracking in "short grain" areas and adds extra thickness to the overall letter.*

more authentic, "woody" look. They also are more adaptable for making clean, router-cut edges.

The short-grain cracking tendencies can be minimized by gluing a thin piece of exterior plywood to the back side of the letter blank (Illus. 77) before sawing out the letter. Use any good exterior, waterproof glue. The thin, exposed plywood edges are hardly noticeable.

The usual steps involved to cut out thick solid wood letters are demonstrated in Illustrations 78–81. Super-large letters (those 24 inches high or greater) are made principally the same way. I believe larger letters require progressively thicker stock—whatever is available and economically practical. Thick and wide planks will usually require lamination (gluing narrow planks edge to edge to increase the width of stock, as in Illustration 82). In some extreme cases, it may also be desirable to increase thickness by gluing boards together face to

*Illus. 78 (top left). When possible, crosscut all letters to equal length (height) before transferring the pattern to the wood. Illus. 79 (top right). Some curves are more easily and uniformly cut by boring than sawing. Illus. 80 (bottom left). Jigsawing on the inside opening of a very thick letter blade. Here the guide and holding attachments of the jigsaw were removed to afford a thicker-than-usual cutting capacity. Illus. 81 (bottom right). Band-sawing is the choice method for all outside cuts on thick stock.*

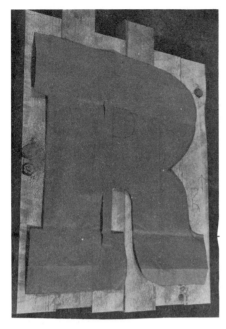

Illus. 82 and 83. Super-large letters (these are all 24 inches high) must be made by gluing pieces together edge to edge. The completed letters, above, were made by gluing narrow pieces of 2-inch stock edge to edge. They were backed with ¼-inch exterior fir plywood. Note the router-cut edges.

face or using ¾-inch-thick plywood as a backing glued to the rear of the letters (Illus. 83).

It is a recommended procedure, when laminating, to rip planks wider than 6 inches in half and then glue the pieces back together. This step relieves internal stresses that might induce future warping. Try to obtain planks that have vertical grain rather than flat grain. Vertical grain does not shrink and swell as much, and tends to warp less. Remember, routing the edges gives a neat, finished look (Illus. 83 and 84). Be sure to finish all exposed surfaces of outdoor letters, including the backs.

**Mounting Letters.** Whenever possible, attach the letters to the sign backing panel with screws or lag bolts driven in from the rear (Illus. 84). Driving fasten-

Illus. 84. These house numbers were glued and screwed (from the rear) to this ¼-inch pre-finished plywood backing, which was then nailed to the house.

*Illus. 85. A stylish application of cutout, shaped, standoff wood lettering. (Designer unknown.)*

ers through the faces of letters should only be done as a last resort. However, there are times when rear mounting is impossible — such as on double-faced signs and when letters are attached to storefronts. In cases like this, there are a few options:

(1) Glue the letters on with waterproof silicone mastics. This is fast, easy, and generally permanent. Indoor sign letters can be "pasted" to the walls with paneling mastic (adhesive) or hot-melt glues.

(2) Use non-corrosive finish nails and exterior glue. If the letters and backing are previously finished, you will not get the maximum holding power of the

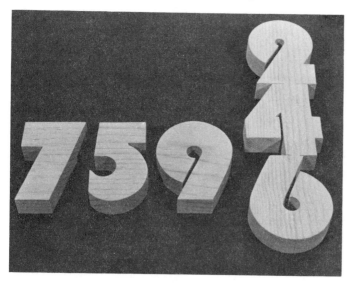

*Illus. 86. Vertically connected house numbers make an interesting departure from the conventional individual numbers that read horizontally.*

*Illus. 87. After a name has been sawn to its normal profile shape on a board of parallel thickness, an unusual name sign can be created by making one diagonal bevel cut.*

glue. Also, if you assemble before finishing, the subsequent painting and staining around the letters will be time-consuming and aggravating.

(3) Use metal fasteners only, going right through the faces of the letters. Countersink the screw or bolt heads. Then plug or fill the holes and finish to match.

**Standoff Letters** are attached the same way (usually as point 3 above), but with some sort of unobtrusive spacing material between the letters and the sign back panel. Standoff, cutout letters give the sign yet an extra dimension of depth. This method casts interesting shadows (Illus. 85) and also makes future staining or painting around the letters much easier than when the letters are mounted directly to the panel. Spacers can be small pieces of wood, dowels, or short lengths of plastic, copper, or brass piping. Avoid using any materials with corrosive or rusting tendencies. Also, don't be excessive — ½ to 2 inches is a suitable range of space, progressively for small to larger signs.

Using cutout letters affords the sign-maker a wide range of material and design options. Letters run together or connected (achieved by overlapping letter patterns) make novel signs. Name signs and house numbers made this way make special personal gifts (Illus. 86 and 87). Let your imagination run wild, and go forth and have fun making signs with cutout letters.

# 5  Hand-Carved Signs

Making hand-carved signs demands more patience and artistic skills than any other form of sign work. However, the extra efforts invested afford the craftsman a far greater reward in pride and personal satisfaction. The range of proficiency in the craft/art will depend upon your technique, ability, and persistence in becoming a woodcarver. As with any form of woodworking, every project (sign) you carve will give you additional experiences that can be helpful and applied to the next piece of work.

Hand-carved wood signs can be separated into two basic categories: (1) *incised carvings* (making incisions) in which the letters (or characters) are cut into the surface (Illus. 88); and (2) *raised or relief* work in which the background surrounding the letters or design is cut away (Illus. 89). Signs may also be crafted to feature both of these techniques in a single work (Illus. 90). Hand-carved signs can simply feature the message in carved lettering, or they can be expanded with auxiliary carved ornaments and decorations, transforming the signs into eloquent works of art (Illus. 90–92). There are only a few woodcarvers around the country involved in commercial wooden sign work. The demand for their skills is quite substantial, and in turn they can demand good fees. However, only those possessing great skill coupled with speed can make suitable hourly wages.

*Illus. 88. An example of incised hand-carved lettering. The rope effect was not carved, but rather purchased as ready-made moulding and attached to the sign.*

*Illus. 89. A sample of raised-letter, or relief, sign-carving.*

Illus. 90 and 91. *Two signs by master-carver Douglas Williams. The one at left features both incised and relief lettering, and the three-dimensional art was attached.*

This chapter will provide "how-to" instructions for the beginner. You will also see inspiring examples of beautiful sign work produced by highly skilled, professional woodcarvers. The techniques for the beginner are essentially the same as those used over and over again by the accomplished professional. The key point is to design and plan your first sign simply. That is, so its level of complexity does not exceed your skills or your patience.

**Tools** required for making hand-carved signs can involve many different shapes and styles of chisels and gouges (available to woodcarvers) or just a simple few. A small set of carving tools (Illus. 93) is more than adequate for beginners, as well as most professionals. It is strongly recommended that at the start you make do with tools you already have. Obtain additional tools one at a

*Illus. 92. This work of professional sign-carver Bill Schnute is an excellent example of relief lettering, as well as beautiful three-dimensional detailing.*

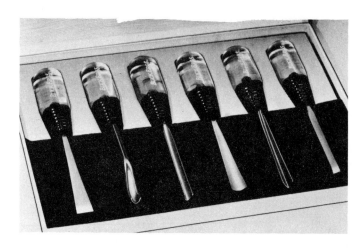

*Illus. 93. A basic set of woodcarving tools.*

time as you determine whether or not you really need them. Many a good sign can be carved with just an ordinary carpenter's chisel, a jackknife, and perhaps a gouge. Having all of the various sizes and shapes of carving tools isn't really as important as you may think. What is of major importance is to be sure that the tools you do have are extremely sharp. This matter cannot be overly stressed. Trying to work with dull tools will discourage a novice faster than anything else. Tools must be "razor-sharp"!

Learning how to carve and properly use the tools can only be achieved by actually carving. So, start with the tool(s) you have, and you will learn and determine if other special tools must be purchased to perfect your own style of sign carving. There are many excellent books that will instruct you about the general and technical aspects of woodcarving. Look at a few books for the additional information you may need, but, most of all, devote your greatest reading and study to the chapters about sharpening tools.

You will find that to become a successful carver you must not only control the tool, but you must also control the response of the wood by anticipating how it will react to your cuts. You must know where and how much you want to cut away. Simply being able to accomplish this should be your first goal. Style, speed, and overall expertise will improve consistently with experience. Selecting good wood for carving is of major importance if you intend to control the wood's reaction to your efforts. At first it's assumed that all softwoods are the easiest to carve. This is by and large true, but softwoods require the sharpest edges—much sharper than for carving harder, denser woods. Dull tools will tear or crush the fibres of softwoods, whereas dull tools will require more force or energy when carving hardwoods. With properly sharpened tools, both softwoods and hardwoods alike will carve surprisingly easily.

In general, walnut, mahogany, basswood, redwood, and pine are good carving woods. For signs, particularly exterior signs, use redwood, mahogany, cedar, sugar pine, or basswood. Always purchase a select or high grade of wood. Be sure that it is free of knots, swirls, or cross grain. Your wood should have straight, uniform grain—especially for your first effort.

**Carving** will initially require continuous concentration with regard to grain direction. Later, this will become instinctive and you will be cutting automatically with the grain—simultaneously controlling the wood's reaction and your cutting tool. Cutting deeper than intended, or having chips come off where you do not want them to, can usually be traced to working against the grain or using dull tools.

**Carving Incised Letters.** The easiest kind of incised (carved-in) letters to make are those that are "V"-cut so the deepest point is at the center of the letter (Illus. 88). Attempting to carve out the total profile of the letter to a uniform depth is a very difficult task. To begin with, select a basic typeface, such as a simple block letter without fancy serifs (decorative tails) (Illus. 88 and 89 as opposed to Illus. 90–92). Plan the sign layout so the letters run the length of the board. That is, so the majority of your cuts will be across the grain. You will find this easier than carving letters in which the grain runs vertically with the height of the letters. Use carbon paper and transfer your layout to the wood. Then draw a center line on each letter to indicate where the deepest cut of the letter will be. End these center lines with uniform triangles drawn at the end of

*Illus. 94 (left). The center-line depth-cut is made first. Here, the gouge used to sever the grain fibres matches the curve of the letter.*

*Illus. 95 (below). The first slant cut begins to make one of the sloping sides of the letter.*

*Illus. 96 (left). The straight "legs" of the letters can be made entirely with a carpenter's wood chisel. Note that the bevel is up for this sloping cut. Illus. 97 (right). Nearing the final depth.*

the leg or the stroke of each character — connecting the center lines to the outside lines. Study the layout in Illustrations 94 and 95.

All woodcarving revolves around only a few basic techniques and kinds of cuts. The basic cuts are: (1) stop cuts (Illus. 94), which involve severing the fibres (usually across the grain), and (2) slicing cuts, which usually involve making cuts at an angle with the grain — moving the tool toward the stop cuts to remove chips (Illus. 95 and 96). Make the center-line depth-cuts first. Use a regular flat

*Illus. 98 (left). A utility knife completes the sloping, tapered cut from the center line to the outside corners. Illus. 99 (right). An ordinary wood chisel can be used to clean up the sloping triangular end-cuts. Note that the bevel is up.*

chisel for straight-line work. Hold it vertically with the cutting edge on the center line and give it a firm blow with a mallet or hammer. The purpose of this cut is to sever the grain fibre. Then, subsequent slicing cuts can be made from each side toward the stop cut. If the stroke of the letter is curved rather than straight, you will need a gouge that matches the curve of the center line, as in Illustration 94.

After the initial stop cuts have been made, make the slanted slicing cuts carefully, lifting out the chips (Illus. 95). Continue the vertical stop cuts, followed by the slicing cuts (Illus. 97) from each side until the desired depth is achieved. End the stroke (or leg) of the letters with triangular incisions. Use a sharp knife or chisel, and slice cut these carefully (Illus. 98 and 99). Taper the cut from the center line toward the outer end points.

Use a sharp knife to clean up the sides of the letters. Make certain that the deepest point is in the center of the letter and that all letters are cut close to a uniform depth. Do not sand the surfaces of the sloping sides. This will round off the sharp edge between the sign surface and the cut surfaces of the letter. Edges should be well defined—sharp and crisp.

Some chisel or gouge marks can be left intentionally to give the authenticity of hand-carved work (Illus. 100). However, if your objective is smoothly surfaced letters (as shown in Illus. 101), then remove all tool marks with light finishing cuts, using very sharp tools and taking the necessary time.

**Carving Raised Letters** (relief work) (as shown in Illus. 89–92 and 102) is done with essentially the same basic cuts used to carve incised letters. In relief work, the object is to remove, to a reasonably uniform depth, the wood surrounding the letters. If your aim is to produce a perfectly smooth, flat, and true background, you are undertaking a tedious and time-consuming job. Leaving tool marks on the background is no sin, as long as the overall appearance suggests uniformity over the entire background. This leaves a very interesting,

*Illus. 100. The tool marks left by the carver, Pudge DeGraff, lend an authentic look and add character to this sign.*

*Illus. 101 (above). An expertly crafted sign, carved about 30 years ago by an old German woodcarver, now deceased. Note the smooth surfaces of the letters.*

*Illus. 102 (right). Relief lettering and art carved in redwood. This sign measures three feet by four feet. (Designed and carved by Bill Schnute.)*

textured surface which serves as an interesting contrast to the smooth, undisturbed surface of the letter face (Illus. 102). Perhaps most important, textured backgrounds are faster and easier.

Begin the carving by outlining the letter with vertical chisel or gouge cuts to sever the grain fibres. These cuts can be made more cleanly and easily (especially in softwoods) if they are not cut exactly vertically, but are made at a consistent, slight angle of about 5 to 10 degrees (Illus. 103). Outside curves can be cut with close, successive passes of a straight-edged chisel. Inside curves can

*Illus. 103. Begin relief work by outlining the letters with slightly off-vertical cuts. Note that the bevel of the chisel faces away from the letter.*

be made with a curved gouge — preferably one with an edge that curves less than the curve of the letter. After the letter has been outlined completely, lift out the background with a chisel (Illus. 104) or gouge (Illus. 105), as appropriate. Always do this with slicing cuts, working with the grain. A bent gouge is helpful in cleaning up the background as shown in Illustration 106, but not absolutely necessary. Study Illustrations 107–110.

*Illus. 104. Lifting out a chip with a regular carpenter's chisel — the bevel is down.*

*Illus. 105. Using a gouge to work away the background.*

*Illus. 106. A bent gouge (or bent chisel) is handy for leveling "tight" background spaces (between letters and so on). Here it is used to texture the background, emphasizing the tool marks.*

Illus. 107–110. Carved redwood signs by Bill Schnute. Note his heavily textured backgrounds and delightful design ideas.

**Carving Round Forms in Relief** can add considerably to the uniqueness of wood signs—be they rounded letter faces, rounded borders, or special designs with rounded edges. A simple practice exercise is shown in Illustration 115. Here the lettering was outlined with a $^3/_{32}$ veining router bit, but it could be hand-cut. The convex face of the letter is being shaped entirely with an ordinary carpenter's wood chisel. However, other chisels, gouges, or knives could be used with the same results. Rounding over relief forms is a fairly easy job. With a little practice and some sanding you will be able to produce shapes similar to the details in Illustrations 113, 116, and 117. Once you round over simple designs you are ready to include more details by making shallow incision cuts on these rounded surfaces to produce simple three-dimensional carvings. With practice, continual effort, and the desire to improve your carving skills, you will soon want to move on to the types of signs sculptured and embellished by professional

*Illus. 111–114. More of Douglas Williams' work for your inspiration.*

carvers such as Bill Schnute and Douglas Williams. Carefully study the hand-carved signs in Illustrations 116 and 117. If you analyze these signs, reducing them to simple individual elements, you will note that they are actually not that complicated or artistic. With care, effort, and the basic techniques described above, you can do it, too.

*Illus. 115. Using a chisel (bevel down, here) on a practice exercise for making convex-faced letters.*

**Some Shortcuts.** So far we have only explored the idea of producing authentic hand-carved signs, that is, those fashioned by physical labor with hand tools. Stock removal can be faster. Use a router, or power rotary tools such as files and burrs driven in drill chucks or flexible shafts. Not only can a lot of roughing-out time be saved, but not much thought needs to be given to grain direction. "V" router bits can be used to rough-in incised carved letters and knock off the outside corners of relief work to be rounded over. Finish all surface cuts with hand chisels and gouges to quickly create the hand-carved look. Similarly, letters can be outlined and deep backgrounds removed with a router when doing relief work. Touch up the surfaces by hand, leaving the tool marks obvious. Carve by machine. Letters and other designs can be copied easily with carving duplicators. (Refer to chapter 7.) Don't pass up the idea of combining hand-

*Illus. 116 (above). How's this for an effectively designed carved wood sign?*

*Illus. 117 (right). This is a truly outstanding sign. At first glance it looks very difficult to execute, but study each character—are they as hard to carve as they seem?*

*Illus. 118 (left). The background was routed away and then the surface was textured with a gouge.*

*Illus. 119 (above). Just two of the hundreds of designs in wood mouldings and ornaments that can be purchased to decorate signs.*

carved work with routed or sandblasted work on the same sign. See Illustration 118 for one very elementary example. Use whatever means you have to get the effect you want without expending excessive time or labor—that is unless your efforts are done strictly as a labor of love.

If after all this you still find yourself not wanting to expend any efforts at all to make wood carved ornaments, buy them. Wood mouldings and decorations in numerous sizes, shapes, and design motifs are available. Simply glue them on. Imagine what you could do with the pre-carved ornaments shown in Illustration 119. Look back at Illustration 88. One word of caution—be sure that embossed carvings that are made of veneers are adequately sealed when used on exterior signs. Otherwise, they may delaminate (separate) unless they were originally manufactured for exterior conditions.

Another idea in this same vein is to be alert for aluminum, brass, or plastic castings of three-dimensional objects. Exterior, serviceable plaques (with flat backs) of birds, eagles, fish, animals, and many other designs are available in most hardware stores. When attached to your wood sign, they might provide just the ornamental touch you are looking for. But, really, don't we all like authentic woodcarvings best?

# 6    Routed Signs

**The** portable electric router, featuring great versatility coupled with high cutting speed, lends itself perfectly to wooden sign work of all kinds and sizes. It takes just a touch of know-how, a little imagination, and a bit of practice. You will quickly have the necessary skills, so there is no limit to what you can do. Very beautiful signs can be cut freehand and/or with the aid of various simple homemade (or inexpensive) guides that direct the router along its intended path.

Small name signs and very large commercial signs are routed in basically the same way (Illus. 120–124). Routed signs can be made with the letters either cut into the surface or raised above. Letters carved into the surface are called *engraved*. Engraved letters can be of uniform or various widths (Illus. 120 and 121). In the latter case, letters are cut by making multiple router passes with narrower bits. A form of engraved lettering is "single stroke" work. In this class of work the width of the letter face is equal to the cutting diameter of the bit. The letter strokes are made in just one cutting pass or single carving "stroke" with the router (Illus. 121–123).

**Raised or Relief** signage has the background cut away. See Illustrations 124 and 125. With a little practice, you can produce relief work with textured backgrounds that look as if they were carved by hand. You may also create other unusual effects of your own—simply by accident, or by plan. Look for other ideas to copy in addition to those shown here.

A specific kind or size of router cannot be recommended because personal needs, preferences, and budgets vary. We all know cheap electric tools will neither last as long nor take the abuse that more expensive ones will. Tools with higher horsepower are heavier than those with less power. If you put your mind

*Illus. 120. An engraved, routed sign. Note how the letter strokes, or legs, vary in width.*

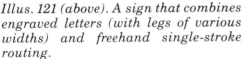

*Illus. 121 (above). A sign that combines engraved letters (with legs of various widths) and freehand single-stroke routing.*

*Illus. 122 (top right). A name sign in single-stroke routing cut with a round-bottom bit.*

*Illus. 123 (bottom right). A big sign executed with a 1-inch-diameter round-bottom bit.*

to it, you can learn to rout signs with any router. As stated in chapter 3, investing in quality router bits is perhaps more important than buying a top-line router. After all, the bits do the cutting. If you intend to go into commercial sign-making, that's another story. However, if you plan just to make a few signs for fun, then use what you have, or what you can rent or borrow. In short, select your router as you would a tool for any woodworking purpose.

One thing I like about my router is the weight. It is big and heavy. Secondly, it has both a pistol-type handle and a knob located low on the base. Thus, I can press my hands and forearms down against the work to maintain good control of the router (Illus. 126). I also like the trigger switch. It's on the handle, so I can use it without moving my grip. My router will also carry two different sizes of collet chucks — ¼ inch and ½ inch. The latter, along with the high-horsepower motor, allows me to use heavier, industrial-quality bits that cut deeper without vibration or chatter.

My router lacked two features which I found a definite need for, and so I added them myself. The first feature is a transparent plastic base (with rounded lower edges) with a large center hole (Illus. 127). I used the factory-made base as a pattern and cut new ones of lexon and polycarbonate plastic. Use tough, clear

*Illus. 124 (left). This routed sign, at a Florida development, makes excellent use of engraved and relief letters with a decorative design. (Designer and fabricator unknown.) Illus. 125 (right). Raised (relief) work, cut entirely with the router using a round-bottom bit, simulates a hand-carved look.*

plastics if you elect to do this, too. Acrylic plastic is a poor choice as it scratches and does not stay clear. Rounding the edges of the base allows the router to glide over slight protrusions and fibres that may be sticking above the surface of a sign-in-progress. The rounded base edges are especially appreciated when I'm routing rough-sawn surfaces and the surfaces of edge-glued panels.

*Illus. 126. The author's router. The clear plastic base and large hole provide easy viewing of the cutting area.*

*Illus. 127. A view of my homemade base. Note the rounded edges.*

The second feature is a vacuum attachment—a powerful, effective one. You cannot continually breathe that fine dust. Moreover, chips, dust, and freed particles get in the way. I devised a crude but workable attachment, hosed directly to my shop vacuum (Illus. 128). I imagine you could use your house vacuum, too. As a matter of convenience my vacuum hangs from the ceiling directly over the workbench, always out of the way.

Connecting the hose to the base unit of the router took a little effort. I cut a sheet-metal pipe-reducer somewhat obliquely to fit alongside of the router base.

*Illus. 128 (left). My homemade vacuum attachment works great, and it is never in the way.*

*Illus. 129 (below). The vacuum connection removed. One knob holds it on.*

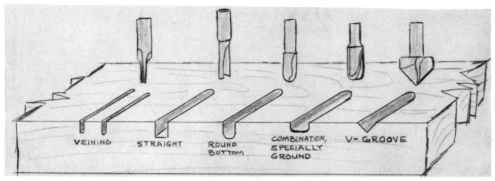

*Illus. 130. Bits and cuts. (See also Illus. 66 on page 34.)*

To get a more airtight fit, epoxy paste was used to fill in the gaps. A generous application of paste wax (with some thin plastic foodwrap) over the router base made a good release, so I did not glue the pipe connection permanently to the router base. I can remove the connection at will and use the router without the vacuum (see Illus. 129). The remaining large gaps between the bridges of the base needed to be closed in to get better suction. This problem was solved with thin, flexible pieces of clear plastic, scissor-cut from goggles lenses. They were simultaneously bent around the curve of the base and glued down fast with hot-melt glue.

So that's my router setup. It works for me, but who knows—I might have been happier with something else. A router with a light that illuminates the work area sounds like a good idea. My shop is well lighted so it's not a serious problem for me. You must always be able to see your layout lines clearly to know where you are cutting. I know several professionals, and they all have different brands and sizes of routers. Each is pleased with his own and wouldn't change—but one thing they all have in common is that they produce great signs.

**Router Bits** should be selected for the shape, size, and kind of cut you intend to make (Illus. 130). If affordable, use carbide when possible. You may at some time want a bit specially ground for you to make certain unusual cuts. Refer to the listings in the Appendix for these services.

**Freehand Routing Engraved Signs** does take some practice, but stick in there—it can be done, and done expertly sooner than you think. At the end of this chapter you will find ideas for some guides that help the router in its work, but sooner or later you will have to take the plunge and try freehand routing.

*Safety First!* Use goggles, ear plugs, respirators, or whatever else necessary to protect your own well-being. Be sure to clamp your work to the bench. Routing is best done as a "sit-down" job. This will save your back. Have an appropriate

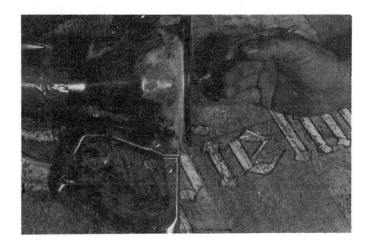

*Illus. 131. A shallow depth and narrow bit are best for the first "crack" at freehand routing. Note that the layout is chalked in to clearly indicate what needs to be cut away.*

seat or stool at a height that allows you to have a good, almost level, "inside" view without straining your back.

Install your bit. Set the depth (Illus. 131). To start your first try, use a shallow depth (about ¼ inch or less) and a narrow straight-bottom bit (¼ inch or less is recommended). Greater depths can be cut with second passes. A shallow start makes router control easier. Stay with shallow depths until you get the feel for various stroke directions and different grain resistances.

Tilt the router, resting it on the base, with the bit clear. Turn on the power and pivot the router downward, dropping the bit into the wood near the layout line. Outline the insides of the letter first, staying well enough away from the layout line in case you are a little "shaky" at the start. You can trim cut up to the line later, after the "meat" of the letter has been removed. Analyze which direction the router tends to go when cuts are directed across, parallel with, and obliquely to, the grain. Study Illustration 132. This drawing indicates the recommended feed directions for making vertical and oblique trimming cuts close to the line. Cutting in directions opposite to those shown may cause the bit to grab and suddenly dig in, forcing you to go beyond the intended line of cut.

The ideal rate or speed with which you move the router varies with bit sharpness, bit diameter, depth of cut, wood hardness, grain, and your eye-hand motor skills. Slowing to a near stop will cause the bit to burn and puff up some smoke. Don't fret! Take it easy and slow, carefully following the lines and gradually speeding up to a suitable feed-speed as you develop confidence and skill.

Be especially careful with small letters like *o*'s, *e*'s and *a*'s, so you don't "kick" cut the center parts. It's for this very reason that small-sized letters are more difficult to do than larger ones. Letters smaller than 1½ inches in height are likely to give you a lot more problems than 2- or 2½-inch letters. Also, with small letters you will need to use narrower bits. When possible, rout from a

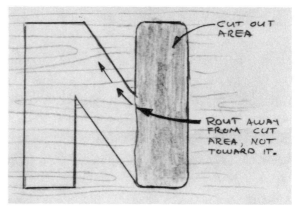

*Illus. 132 (left). The recommended feed directions for trimming (finish) cuts are shown by straight arrows. Bit rotation is indicated by circular arrows. Note that the grain is running horizontally. Illus. 133 (right). When possible, feed away from previously cut areas, not toward them.*

previously cut area toward new wood. Routing toward and into an already cutout area is likely to cause the router to surge, and chipping or breaking off at "short grain" areas will result. See Illustration 133. For letters such as *T*'s, *L*'s and *E*'s, do the vertical strokes of the letters first, moving the router perpendicular to the grain direction. Finish the horizontal "bars" of the letters going with the grain. This procedure will minimize chipping at intersections. More examples of engraved letter work are shown in Illustrations 134–137.

*Illus. 134 (left). An engraved initial plaque with routed edge. Illus. 135 (right). Engraved directional sign. Notice the dovetailed arm post.*

*Illus. 136 (left). A beautiful application of engraved routing. Note the effect given by outlining the leaves with a shallower cut. (Artist-Craftsman unknown.)*

*Illus. 137 (right). Old English engraved freehand with a 3/16-inch flat-bottom bit.*

**Freehand Single Stroke.** In this class of work, letters are made quickly with one straight-line or smooth-flowing, curved stroke. Each stroke component (leg or curve of the letter) is completed with just one pass of the router. For example, the vertical of the letter *D* is made with one straight vertical stroke (top to bottom). The router is lifted and moved to the top and the curve of the letter is completed with a second single pass. Some examples of single-stroke routed signs are shown in Illustrations 138–142. Once skilled at this, you can rout a small sign in 3 or 5 minutes. This skill will come with practice.

*Illus. 138. A freehand, single-stroke routed sign. Lettering was cut with a round-bottom bit, and the art was cut with a V-bit.*

*Illus. 139. This small business sign was routed freehand.*

A less rigid style of lettering is the best to start with. See Illustration 143 for a suggested style. Note that all of the straight cuts are not perfectly straight and the curves are not uniform compass-type curves. A good layout, however, is still essential—especially for the beginner. You can enlarge the letters by any of the methods described in chapter 2. However, with some effort you can learn to lay out this style of lettering without any problems. Simply use chalk and the "trial

*Illus. 140 (left). Single-stroke lettering looks good on rustic signs. Note the wood bracket.*

*Illus. 141 and 142 (above). House number and name sign made by single-stroke, freehand routing.*

B

C

D

AABCDEEFG
HIJKLLLMMN
OPQRRSSTUV
WWXYZ
1234567890

ABCDEFGH
IJKLMNOPQ
RSTUVWX
YZ&
1234567890

*Illus. 143. Alphabets for single-stroke routing. The single-line, freestyle letters are easy to lay out and rout freehand. The double-line letters require more skill.*

*Illus. 144. A chalked layout has been outlined in pencil for freehand, single-stroke routing.*

and error" method. Lightly chalk it on, and if it does not look right or is not centered, wipe it off with a dry rag and do it again, making the necessary adjustments. Once you get it spaced out to a good looking layout, darken and widen the chalk letters to a suitable width. Then outline the chalk lines freehand with pencil. See Illustration 144. Select a router bit of the approximate corresponding diameter.

I prefer to use the round bottom or cove bits for freehand single-stroke work. This type of bit allows me to smooth out a bumpy or irregular curve as well as improve and smooth out straight lines. Of course, this requires making another pass over the same part of the letter, but I would rather do that than let a sloppy job go by. This slightly increases the width of the letter face at the corrected area. Unless it's extremely bad in the first place, the corrected letter is usually

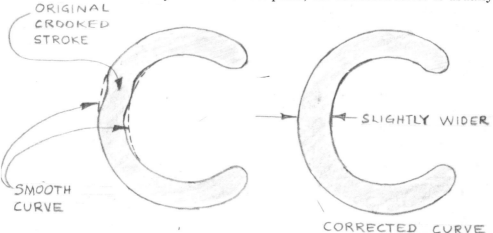

ORIGINAL CROOKED STROKE

SMOOTH CURVE

SLIGHTLY WIDER

CORRECTED CURVE

*Illus. 145. A bad cut can usually be corrected, as shown, by carefully reworking it. Feather the correction-cut into the lines of the original stroke.*

66

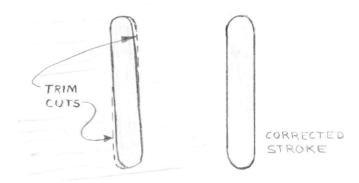

*Illus. 146. Top-to-bottom single-stroke cuts tend to pull to the right. The method for correcting poor verticals is shown here.*

undistinguishable from the others. See Illustrations 145 and 146. With more experience and practice, you will have less correcting to do.

You will find it best to press down on the router handles and reduce the speed of feed when you anticipate the router might be pulled from your intended direction. This is likely to occur around or when going through knots, heartwood to sapwood, other changes of grain direction, and just before coming into another cut. See Illustration 147. You will learn to use your wrists as "compass arms." You will soon be able to let the router basically glide itself "downhill" *with* the grain, and restrain it with just the right pressure as you move it "uphill" *against* the grain. The same old principles are involved in most all forms of routed sign work—practice and more practice!

Freehand single stroke routing with V-groove bits (Illus. 148) requires greater skill because corrections, if necessary, are more noticeable. Unless you increase the depth of cut, a "telltale" inverted "V" (as drawn in Illus. 149) will appear at

*Illus. 147. Freehand, single-stroke routing. Note that the work is firmly clamped down and is completely on the bench to allow the forearm and wrist to control the router.*

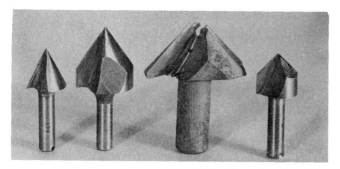

*Illus. 148. V-bits with different angles and diameters. The two on the left were specially ground.*

the center of the letter. Consequently you cannot widen the edges of the letter stroke one at a time. Both must be done with one new stroke and the bit set deeper. Remember, the deeper the cut, the more difficult it is to maintain control. Most sign carvers use redwood when using V-bits. Its easy cutting and very uniform grain are more consistent from piece to piece than any other wood. An advantage of a V-bit is that the cutting width can be changed quickly by raising or lowering the depth of cut. Hence, a different bit need not be installed with every change. Very professional effects with serifs and decorative swirls (swashes) on the ends of letters can be produced (Illus. 150–152). These are made by lifting the router as you complete the stroke. To accomplish this requires not only router practice, but also a knowledge of type styles to which this effect is suitable.

**Routing Guides and Helpful Devices.** If you have come this far without mastering the ups and downs of freehand work, do not despair. There are some homemade and inexpensive devices that can be used to help you make beautiful engraved and raised letters.

**A Straightedge** is the simplest of all guides. Although a true straight line is perhaps the most difficult to cut freehand, it's a "snap" when the router is pushed along a straightedge. The straightedge must be clamped or nailed parallel to the line of cut. Locate the straightedge a distance from the line of cut that

*Illus. 149. This inverted "V" will result if correction cuts are made with a V-bit.*

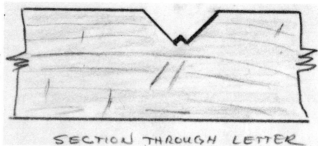

SECTION THROUGH LETTER

Illus. 150 (top). A truly professional job of single-stroke freehand routing in redwood. (Crafted by the Old Oak Shop.) Illus. 151 (left). A close-up look at the "tail" shows that the cut gradually becomes shallower at the end of the stroke. Illus. 152 (right). Another sign by the Old Oak Shop. Note the simulated checks and end-splits cut with a "V" bit. The art was outlined with shallow cuts then artistically hand painted.

equals the distance from the router bit's cutting edge to the edge of the router base (see Illus. 153 and 154). So you don't have to always measure this distance, rip a "spacer-stick" from ¼-inch or ⅛-inch hardboard or plywood (Illus. 153). Use the spacer-stick to line up the straightedge the appropriate distance from the

Illus. 153. A "spacer-stick" is ripped to a width equaling the distance between the bit's cutting edge and the edge of the router base.

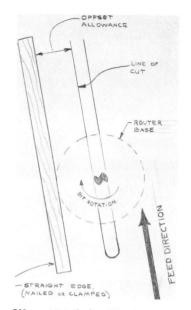

*Illus. 154 (left). The location of the straightedge as it is positioned along the line of cut. Note the recommended direction of feed. Illus. 155 (right). Positioning the straightedge with the help of the "spacer-stick."*

line of cut as shown in Illustration 155. The proper feed direction of the router is important. Feed the router from the direction that tends to pull the router toward the straightedge. This is shown in the drawing, Illustration 154. When feeding in the direction opposite to that shown, the rotation direction of the router bit tends to force the router away from the straightedge. This tendency, of

*Illus. 156 (left). Making a cut by following the straightedge assures that the line of this letter will be perfectly straight. Illus. 157 (right). Here the straightedge, nailed to the sign, assures that all letters will be cut to identical heights.*

*Illus. 158 (left). A T-square designed for guiding the router. Here a "spacer-stick" is used to position the T-square properly along the line of cut. Illus. 159 (right). The T-square is used here to make true vertical cuts for the outline of a large letter.*

course, can be overcome with physical pressure, but you must apply pressure continuously throughout the entire cut.

Use the straightedge for uniform alignment in cutting the tops and bottoms of all letters that have straight line strokes (Illus. 156 and 157).

**A T-Square Guide** is another easily made fixture. It is used to make straight line vertical cuts in letters that are perpendicular to the bottom or base line. The device simply consists of two parallel straightedges (¼ inch in thickness) spaced equally apart at a distance that equals the diameter of the router base plus $1/64$ inch for clearance. The "head" of the T-square is made of ¾-inch plywood so it can hook over the bottom edge of the sign (study Illus. 158 and 159). This double straightedge T-square guide allows you to feed the router in either direction

*Illus. 160 (left). The straight-line slanted legs of letters can be cut in the same manner with the T-square guide firmly clamped. Illus. 161 (right). Once all of the straight-line horizontal and vertical cuts have been made with the straightedge and T-square, the curved cuts must be completed freehand.*

*Illus. 162. A completed sign in which all straight lines were cut with the aid of a straightedge and T-square. Other cuts were made strictly freehand.*

without fear of the router straying away from the line of cut. When clamped securely, the straight-line angle cuts of *N*'s, *A*'s, and so on, can be made without problems (Illus. 160). The remaining curved strokes of the letters must be completed freehand (see Illus. 161 and 162).

**Routing Perfect Circles** is especially difficult to do freehand. Often large signs require true circular cuts with a uniform radius, such as those shown in Illustrations 163 and 164. This kind of work can be done easily if you simply make a compass out of your router. The device consists only of one piece of ¼-inch hardboard (or plywood) made to fit onto the base of the router as shown

*Illus. 163 (left). The perfect circular design on this sign was cut with the aid of a compass routing device. Illus. 164 (right). All of the curved cuts of this logo are perfectly circular and were made with the simple device shown in Illus. 165–168.*

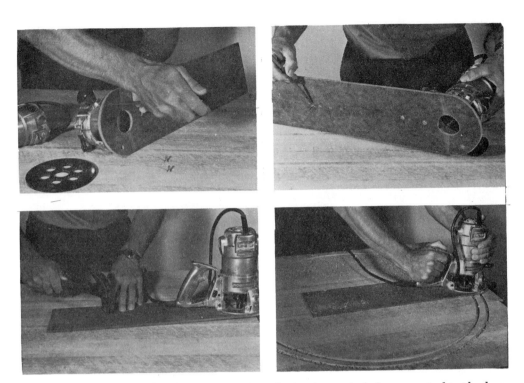

*Illus. 165 (top left). The compass cutting device is made to be mounted to the base of the router. Illus. 166 (top right). A nail makes the pivot point for the center of the circle. Position the nail so the radius of the cut is from the outside of the bit's cutting edge. Illus. 167 (bottom left). Drive in the nail at the center of the circle. Illus. 168 (bottom right). Making perfect circular cuts. Note that parallel circular cuts can be made easily.*

in Illustration 165. Use a nail for the compass pivot point (Illus. 166). Set the nail at the center of the circle, tap it in, and make the cut feeding from either direction (Illus. 167 and 168).

**Letter Routing with Templates.** Engraved and raised letters or other characters (including perfect small and large circles) can be made simply by tracing templates with the router. The templates can either be purchased or made yourself from ¼-inch plywood or hardboard. One item you need is a template routing guide (hollow bushing) that fits into the center hole of your standard router base (Illus. 169). Most router manufacturers provide these in sets with various size openings so you can use bits with various cutting diameters. The template guide bushing protrudes through the bottom of the plastic router base and bears against the letter template during the routing operation.

*Illus. 169 (left). A close-up view of a homemade letter template and the relationship of the template guide and the router bit. Illus. 170 (right). Templates nailed in place for making raised letters.*

*Illus. 171. A template holding device for routing engraved letters. Sold by Sears, this setup has 58 plastic templates with heights of 2¾ inches and 1¾ inches, and it comes with a clamping system.*

To make raised letters, nail the template directly to the sign (Illus. 170). Once you have installed the proper combination of router bit and template guide bushing, set the bit to the desired depth. *Caution:* Be careful when lowering the rotating bit into the work. Be sure you do not accidentally cut the template with the bit. Follow along with slight horizontal pressure so the template guide always rides against the template during the outlining operation. Turn off the router and wait for the bit to coast down to a complete stop before lifting the router.

The same general idea can be employed to make engraved letters. Or, you can purchase a template set made especially for this type of work, as shown in Illustration 171.

# 7  Sign Routing and Carving Machines

This chapter briefly describes some of the dozen or so sign-making machines currently available on the market. Most equipment of this type is based upon a template-guided router which reproduces the exact letter shapes of the master patterns. They are, in fact, copying machines. They can be operated without any previous woodworking experience and do not require any special artistic skills. The machines vary in price, ranging between fifty and several thousand dollars. In most cases, the templates, guides, bits, and other accessories are extra, and with some machines the buyer must also provide or purchase the router power unit separately.

Any bit carried by a conventional portable router can be used with this type of equipment. Round, square-bottom, or V-bits are used to produce various signs. Letters and/or decorations are either carved into the surface (engraved) or raised by cutting away all of the background. Some manufacturers offer very complete sets of templates in a variety of type styles with upper and lower case letters, spacers, numerals, special characters, and even three-dimensional design motifs. Some companies do not have any templates or lettering guides available, in which case you must make your own.

The machines vary in their maximum sign-size capacities. They also have certain other limitations, as well as distinctly individual construction features. Before purchasing any machine or device, it would be wise to contact each manufacturer (names and addresses are listed in the Appendix) and make your own comparative study of their literature.

**The Kimball "Woodcarver"** (Illus. 172) is a tabletop-size unit, measuring 48 inches wide, 32 inches deep, and 20 inches high. It has an aluminum housing construction, with a 175-pound gross weight. This machine carries a standard portable electric router and any ¼-inch shank router bit can be used. It has provision for a dust-collection attachment which connects to a shop vacuum collection tank.

The carriage is of ball-bearing construction. It has a 1-to-1 ratio movement with an easily controlled stylus that reproduces actual size by following supplied templates that are made of clear plastic. The manufacturer has a wide range of templates available. They include alphabets in block, script, and old English, and other various designs (ships, fish, animals, etc.). The actual cutting can involve either outlining from the template shapes or full removal (silhouetting).

*Illus. 172. The Kimball woodcarving machine.*

The machine can also be used "freehand" to carve letters or other artwork by following pencil drawings with the stylus. Cutout letters and templates can also be made on this machine, as well as three-dimensional carvings or other designs that can be carved into the wood. Illustrations 173–176 show the range of work that can be done with the Kimball woodcarving machine.

*Illus. 173 (top left). Examples of letter styles routed with the Kimball machine.*
*Illus. 174 (bottom left). Cutout letters and template patterns can also be made with the machine. Illus. 175 (right). Close-up of engraved work possible.*

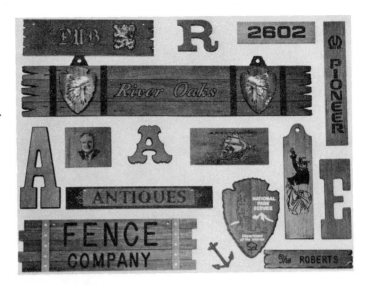

*Illus. 176. A variety of sign designs and art work made with the Kimball carver.*

**The Marlin Carving Machine** (Illus. 177) is another duplicator that reproduces on a 1-to-1 ratio from templates and other full-size patterns. Marlin Industries offers three different models, each with a different carving range—the largest being 22 × 28 inches. However, signs of any (unlimited) length can be cut with their machines. The Marlin machines all function on the pantograph principle. The router bit will copy any object or contoured surface the tracing stylus follows. Their largest machine requires approximately 54 × 60 inches of table or bench space. It has a shipping weight of 55 pounds without the router motor (which the customer can provide himself). The router motor unit must be 3½ inches in diameter, otherwise it will not fit in the router arm mounting.

*Illus. 177. The Marlin carving machine in operation. The operator guides the tracing stylus in the letter template groove as the router bit reproduces the letter.*

Illus. 178–180. Three signs produced with the Marlin sign-carving machine. The sign on the right illustrates the potential of the machine. Note the raised letters and textured background.

Examples of sign work produced with a Marlin machine are shown in Illustrations 178–180.

**The Dupli-Carver** is a similar router-cutting, three-dimensional carving device, manufactured by Laskowski Enterprises. The company offers several models in different sizes. Their carving and duplicating machines will reproduce ready-made signs or cut new signs from template patterns. One special feature

Illus. 181. Producing a sign on a three-dimensional carving machine by duplicating the master pattern. Notice the surface texture and engraved lettering.

*Illus. 182. The Sears "Rout-a-Signer."*

is a bit guard which doubles as a handle (see Illus. 181). With this machine, as with the others described, three-dimensional carvings or other objects can be copied to add decorative touches to signs having engraved or raised letter work.

**The Rout-A-Signer** (Illus. 182) produces engraved, slanted (about 28 degrees), block letters. This sign-making machine (available at Sears outlets) is adjustable, producing letter sizes from ¾ inch to 4½ inches in height. It must be combined with your own router. Signs of any length can be made, but stock is limited to 10 inches in width and boards ½ to 2 inches thick. In operation, plastic templates are traced with a stylus which, by means of a steel bar linkage, moves the router.

It comes partially assembled, with operating instructions and 58 templates of 1½- and 2½-inch numerals and uppercase block letters in a plastic storage carousel. No template guide (bushing) is required for the router base. The router adapter (to which your router is attached) is made of polystyrene plastic. Other parts are steel. The total weight is approximately 10 pounds. The overall size, assembled, is 30 × 22 inches, and 2½ inches high.

**The Sears Router Pantographs** (Illus. 183–186) are inexpensive devices designed to accept any kind of router. They can copy many patterns and templates, but in any of three reduced sizes (40, 50, and 60 percent reduction of

*Illus. 183 (left). A full view of a pantograph, a router accessory offered by Sears. Here, paper patterns are traced to carve letters in a reduced size. Illus. 184 (right). A close-up view of the Sears deluxe router pantograph. The work piece is secured with wedges, and a regular router is attached to the slotted base with adjustable wing nuts and clamps.*

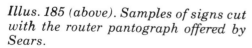

*Illus. 185 (above). Samples of signs cut with the router pantograph offered by Sears.*

*Illus. 186 (right). Here, the Sears router pantograph proportionally reduces a plaster pattern for a three-dimensional wood sign decoration.*

the master pattern). The maximum size pattern is limited to 9 × 12 inches. Changing from one reduction ratio to another is accomplished by repositioning the router on the fixture (Illus. 184). Your router is simply clamped to the appropriate location with clips secured by wing nuts. The manufacturer suggests that you make your own mounting base (fixture) from ½ × 20 × 48-inch plywood to effect a portable unit. However, it could be permanently mounted to a bench or tabletop as well.

Once set up, little practice is needed to guide the stylus along the pattern lines. In operation, you do not hold the router—just the handlebars of the stylus. Straight line cuts reproduced from paper drawings (or patterns) are best accomplished by guiding the stylus along a straightedge held firmly on top of the pattern.

This type of routing aid comes with instructions, clamping wedges, and patterns (stencils) for numbers and the five lettering styles shown in Illustration 185. An additional feature of this router accessory, as with most of those described in this chapter, is the capability of making three-dimensional flat-back carvings. With the Sears Pantograph, patterns up to 12 × 24 inches and 1¼ inches thick can be reproduced into 3-D wood carvings (Illus. 186). When glued on, they add decorative embellishments to routed wood signs. Inexpensive plaster and plastic plaques make good patterns for this type of three-dimensional carving work. These are usually available at most hardware, crafts, and department stores.

# 8  Making Large Signs

Larger signs are laid out, routed, handcarved, or sandblasted the same way as smaller signs. The problems associated with making larger signs include (1) making or preparing large panels, which requires some equipment, (2) making joints, and (3) using fasteners that are required to assemble signs and hand them on buildings or from posts.

As mentioned in an earlier chapter, plywood can often be used for the background panels of large signs. Plywood does not lend itself to hand carving or sandblast carving. Sometimes, however, plywood can be used for signs that are to be engraved with the router, providing you use carbide bits. Large sheets of plywood framed with solid wood borders add to the depth and overall rigidity of the sign. Some ways of making borders for plywood panels are shown in Illustration 187.

When solid lumber is glued together to make large sign panels, it is seldom framed unless the framing members are part of the sign-post assembly (Illus. 188). If edge-to-edge glued sign panels of solid wood are to be framed, be sure to allow space for expansion. Otherwise, the corner joints of your frame may separate. See Illustration 189. As a general rule, avoid framing large edge-glued panels because of wood's tendency to expand and contract with changes in environmental humidity. See Illustration 190.

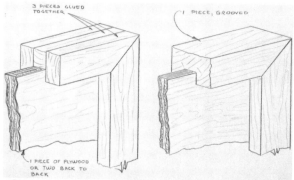

Illus. 187 (above). Making borders for plywood signs.

Illus. 188 (right). This large sign (6-foot-square face) is made of edge-glued 2-inch-thick planks, set and glued into grooves cut into 6-inch-by-6-inch timbers.

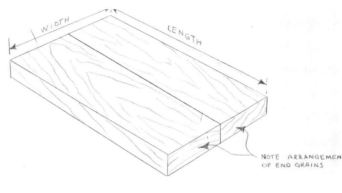

*Illus. 189. Solid wood glued edge to edge to make large sign panels. Remember that wood swells (and shrinks) considerably in width and very little in length.*

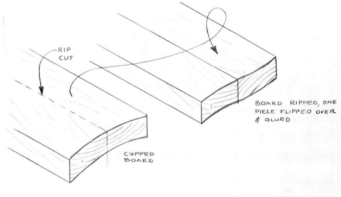

*Illus. 190. Wide planks tend to warp or are warped at the start. Ripping and then gluing them back together makes them stay flatter.*

**Preparing and Gluing Panels** for larger signs involve some generally common woodworking practices. Begin by selecting your lumber for boards of uniform thickness. Incidentally, 2-inch thickness is best for large signs. If the sign is to have a smooth surface, you will get the best results if the boards are all run through a thickness planer. If only one face of the sign needs to be left with a rough-sawn surface, then these boards also can be run through the thickness planer, removing stock from the least desirable face or side of each board. Before surfacing rough-sawn wood, it is a good idea to touch-sand it (Illus. 191). Arrange the boards so that defects, such as knots, end up away from the lettering area. Once arranged, chalk a triangle onto the face sides (Illus. 192). This will enable you to get them back quickly into the predetermined sequence. Smooth and square the edges with a power jointer or carefully with a hand plane.

If the sign boards are longer than 2 feet, they should be doweled in their joints. The purpose of doweling is more a matter of alignment than adding strength to the joint. Often, long boards will be bowed along their length. The dowels used in edge-to-edge gluing will bring each edge into alignment with the edge of the board next to it, and will also keep the edges in the proper positions

*Illus. 191. Touch-sanding rough-sawn surfaces improves the surfaces for planing, gluing, and subsequent routing. The sanding levels fibres and other irregularities, especially around knots.*

until clamping pressure is applied. This will assure a flat, uniform sign face. Doweling begins by drawing lines across the dowel locations (about 6 to 12 inches apart) along the edges of the adjoining boards, as shown in Illustration 193. Use a dowel jig to assure that the dowel holes are drilled vertically and are exactly centered across the edge (Illus. 194 and 195). (See the Appendix for sources of dowel jigs.)

On signs that have rough-sawn surfaces, it may be desirable to emphasize the joint. This is accomplished by making a slight chamfer cut along each board edge on the face side. The result is a neat inverted "V" when the joint is brought together, as shown in Illustration 196. This chamfer cut also assures that the router base will slide easily, without interference, over the joint. Often, the edge of a board is slightly higher (or lower) than the board next to it, as shown in

*Illus. 192. Gluing arrangement of the planks is marked with a triangle to identify the gluing order.*

*Illus. 193 (top left). Marking for dowels is best done by drawing the line on both edges of the joint at the same time. Illus. 194 (bottom left). A self-centering dowel jig. A mark on the jig corresponds to the center of the dowel hole. Illus. 195 (right). A wooden block under the chuck assures that all holes will be drilled to the proper depth.*

Illustration 197. Problems can arise when you are routing sign faces that have these irregular surfaces. Usually the router base strikes a high edge and causes a frustrating miscue. Uneven surfaces, such as shown in Illustration 197, can be sanded down only if the sign is to have a completely smooth face. The chamfering operation is shown in Illustration 198.

*Illus. 196. A slight chamfer, cut at the edge and face-corners of each board, will emphasize the glue joint and make routing easier.*

*Illus. 197. If uncham-
fered edges stick up,
routing is more dif-
ficult.*

Glues for exterior signs should be selected very carefully. Too much work goes into signs of this type to have them ruined just because the wrong glue was used. A resorcinol-resin glue is often recommended for completely waterproof glue joints. It comes as a liquid and a powder, and must be measured carefully and mixed together. It leaves a distastefully wide and reddish, discoloring stain along the glue lines. It's also expensive. I don't like it and can't understand why it is always "the" recommended glue. I use a marine-grade, powdered, plastic resin glue formulated for boat builders. It is manufactured by the Wilhold Company and is available from the sources listed in the Appendix. It leaves a glue line that is almost colorless and barely detectable. It is much less expensive than any resorcinol I have priced. It has a long shelf life (in a tightly closed container), it sets in 4 hours, cures overnight, and can be used at a lower temperature than resorcinol. This Wilhold glue mixes with water and, before it sets, it can be cleaned up with water. Epoxy glue is very good. It's messy to work

*Illus. 198. The chamfer-
ing operation can be
done with a piloted
chamfering router bit
(as shown) or with a
hand plane.*

86

*Illus. 199 (left). Spreading the glue. Illus. 200 (right). After the glue has been spread, drive dowels into one board of the joint. No special effort need be made to get the glue on the dowels or into the holes.*

with and expensive. Epoxy and resorcinol glues adhere even when wood is submerged at length in boiling water. However, how often do you soak your signs in boiling water?

Spread the glue (of your choice) to the edges (Illus. 199) and drive in the dowels (Illus. 200). Don't waste time trying to get glue on the dowels and into the dowel holes. Remember the dowels are only used to assist the alignment in assembly. Dowels add little strength to the joint. Most woodworkers will tell you that the glue joint is stronger than the wood itself. Apply clamping pressure (Illus. 201). A good joint should have some glue squeeze out. However, be careful when working with rough-sawn planks. Excessive glue will be difficult to get off. Use a putty knife (Illus. 202) to lift and clean the squeezed-out glue from the joint area. This is generally easy if you have the V-groove at the joint. See Illustration 203. A very light sanding, after the glue has cured, will make an excellent routing surface. Obviously, if you are using smoothly surfaced planks, most of the above procedures and precautions need not apply.

*Illus. 201 (left). A sign glued and clamped. Note the use of clamps both above and below the sign. The scrap blocks under the clamp jaws distribute pressure and prevent crushing at clamping points. Illus. 202 (right). Lifting the excess glue from the V-joint of a sign assembled from rough-sawn edge-glued planks.*

*Illus. 203. Final cleanup is made with a damp rag.*

Sometimes you may elect to use steel rods (continuously threaded) running through the sign to pull the boards tightly together (edge to edge). These are available in all hardware stores. Use those that are zinc plated and the same for the washers and nuts. Reinforcing your sign with steel rods is a good idea, especially if the sign is to be a free-hanging type (Illus. 204 and 205). The steel rods will keep the pieces of wood together should one of the boards eventually split lengthwise. Running steel rods is more difficult than it first seems. The holes must be drilled exactly through the center. If a hole is slightly off, or if one of the boards is cupped, you may create a seriously distorted and bowed face when drawing the nuts up tight. A dowel drilling jig is often helpful for starting perfectly centered holes. Drill in from both edges of each board, going as deeply

*Illus. 204 (left). A free-hanging sign made of three pieces of rough-sawn wood, joined edge to edge. Illus. 205 (right). This double-faced sign measures about 3½ feet in diameter. It is made of smooth-faced wood with eyebolts coupled to steel rods that run vertically through the sign.*

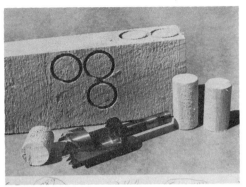

*Illus. 206 (above). This special tool is handy for counterboring operations.*

*Illus. 207 (right). This plug cutter makes dowel pins from scrap. They can be made with grain running either way.*

as you can with the dowel drilling jig. Usually it is a good idea to counterbore a large hole about 1½ inches deep at the outside edge. This will allow you to hide the washer and nut with a wood plug, dowel, or wood filler. See Illustrations 206 and 207.

Screw eyes or lag hooks are used to hang small and medium-sized signs. The bigger the sign, the bigger the fasteners you need. Remember, fasteners driven into the board's end grain do not hold very well. Consequently, signs to be hung, such as those shown in Illustrations 208 and 209, should have a suitable anchor.

*Illus. 208 (above). Hanging this thick, heavy sign will require well-anchored hooks on the top.*

*Illus. 209 (right). A sign to be hung. The screw eyes are driven into the end grain of the vertical planks.*

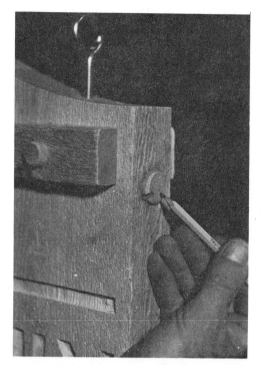

*Illus. 210 (left). This dowel (glued) makes a strong anchor for the screw eye above, which is driven into it. Illus. 211 (right). The sign planks are fastened from the face to the posts with hidden lag bolts. Dowel plugs conceal the bolts and add to the overall character of this rustic sign.*

*Illus. 212 (left). This large single-faced sign is 4 inches thick, and measures about 36 inches by 72 inches. It is glued, lagged, and plugged to two 8-by-8 posts. Illus. 213 (right). These planks are attached to the posts with lag screws, which are concealed by plugs inserted flush to the surface.*

*Illus. 214 (left). A single-faced sign can be mounted directly to the post.*

*Illus. 215 (right). A post with a horizontal arm for hanging a sign must be strongly constructed so it does not sag.*

Since screws hold better when inserted across the grain rather than with the grain, use a large dowel anchor as shown in Illustration 210.

Often the sign boards and blanks need to be fastened directly to posts, as shown in Illustrations 211 and 212. They can be fastened directly from the face side. The fasteners can be concealed with plugs to give a pegged effect (Illus. 211 and 212) or concealed with flush plugs (Illus. 213).

*Illus. 216. A round pole that has been flattened on two sides makes an interesting post for this double-faced sign.*

*Illus. 217 (left). A post structure for a large sign is made with simple lap joints, bolted together.*

*Illus. 218 (right). Four-by-fours cut so the sign panel comes through to the outside make an easy-to-build but substantial-looking post system.*

Posts for small name signs can be made in several ways. Three different ideas are shown in Illustrations 214–216. These pictures are essentially self-explanatory as far as construction details are concerned. Posts for any kind of sign should be of a material that has a high resistance to decay, such as redwood, cedar, cypress, or pressure-treated timbers. In cold areas of the country where frost lift can be a problem, be sure that the post(s) is long enough, and the hole

*Illus. 219 and 220. Two views of an interesting sign in Florida. Note the low sign and the decorative use of round poles, which have been left at random heights, as posts. The close-up of the sign face shows the effectiveness of lettering routed to two different depths. (Designer and fabricator unknown.)*

*Illus. 221 (left). The post structure not only supports the informative sign but also "frames" the entrance to this park. Illus. 222 (right). This unusual sign features sandblasted designs on the posts, which are made of two large planks. (Designer and fabricator unknown.)*

dug deep enough, to get below frost line. If you plan to cement the post(s) in, make your hole with a larger diameter at the bottom of the hole than at the top. This sort of dovetails the post and concrete into the ground. Consequently, it will be much more difficult for the frost to lift it out.

Posts for larger, commercial-type signs should be of a suitable proportional size so they are not overbearing, yet appear to be strong enough, and are strong enough. Some thought must be given to the best height for the sign. Consider ditches, future weeds, or brush growing up in front of the sign. In northern areas, deep snows and plowed banks could cover sign faces if the signs are

*Illus. 223 (left). The face and ends are tongue-cut and set into vertical grooves routed into the posts. The sign is high enough to remain uncovered by deep Wisconsin snows.*

*Illus. 224 (right). The extra posts give needed mass for the visual sense of support and strength.*

*Illus. 225. Smooth redwood sign and sculpture complemented with stone. Sign is 6 inches thick and measures 12 inches by 14 feet. The sculpted design is 12½ feet long and its thickest point is 2½ feet.*

*Illus. 226 (left). A sign designed for portability. The customer wanted to be able to move the sign without leaving postholes in the blacktop parking lot.*

*Illus. 227 (right). Large, heavy hanging signs must be anchored to prevent wind sway. Six-inch-square posts support this sign which is securely chained at top and bottom.*

installed too close to the ground. One of the easiest post systems to fabricate is shown in Illustration 217. Multiple posts can add greatly to the overall design effect. See Illustrations 218–227 for some post designs and construction ideas for supporting large signs.

# 9    Making a Huge Sign

This chapter will present a picture and caption story of the major steps involved to produce a very, very large sign. This one example is included to offer proof that there is virtually no limit to wooden sign work. How big is big enough to be considered "huge" is perhaps a matter of opinion. However, the sign fabricated in this chapter has the following general specifications: the sign face is 7½ feet wide by 10½ feet high and it is 4½ inches thick (solid). It takes six men to lift the sign alone. The sign post structure consists of 2800 board feet of timbers. The timbers are set 4 feet below ground level and anchored with 11 cubic yards of concrete. I considered it a huge sign and a huge undertaking for my small shop. The pictures tell the story.

The size of this job and equipment involved appear at first more than you want to undertake. However, the extra tools (clamps, etc.) can often be borrowed or rented. You can also find someone to sub-contract the work that you cannot handle yourself. Ask around for help before turning down the opportunity to do a challenging and satisfying job such as shown here. Remember, making a huge sign involves the same principles as a small sign—it just takes longer and everything is on a larger scale.

*Illus. 228. The sign just after it was hung. It measures 4½ inches thick, 7½ feet by 10½ feet. The sign is double-faced and is router-carved with raised lettering. Twenty-eight hundred board feet of hand-hewn posts (4 feet below ground) support the structure along with 11 cubic yards of concrete.*

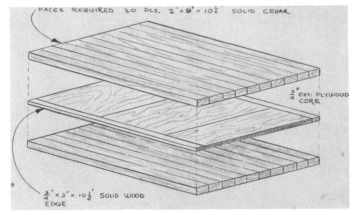

FACES REQUIRED 20 PCS. 2" x 9" x 10½ SOLID CEDAR

⅜" EXT. PLYWOOD CORE

¾" x 3" x 10½' SOLID WOOD EDGE

*Illus. 229. The sign face is all glue-laminated with edge-to-edge glued planks. The thickness is built up with an exterior-grade plywood core with solid wood for the core edges.*

*Illus. 230. The face panels. The first (standing) is already glued and cut, and the second panel (in long pipe-clamps) is being edge-to-edge glued on the workbench.*

*Illus. 231. Leveling the gluing surfaces by cross-grain sanding.*

*Illus. 232. The profile shape cuts are made before glue-up. The one face is used as a pattern to cut the second face.*

*Illus. 233. The hanger eyes are imbedded and anchored to the interior of the sign during glue-up. This ¾-inch-diameter steel rod and eye is welded to a steel plate (⅜ inch thick, 3 inches by 16 inches), screwed and epoxy-paste-glued into the pocket cut into the ¾-inch plywood core.*

*Illus. 234. Preparing the glue on the last face. At this point the core has already been glued and nailed to one face. Note the solid wood at the edges of the core.*

*Illus. 235 (left). Clamps are placed around the outside edges. The total thickness was completed in a single glue-up. Illus. 236 (right). A total view of the thickness glue-up. Timbers are wedged against the ceiling to apply pressure to the center of the sign—pressing it to the workbench.*

*Illus. 237. Sign laid out, ready for routing —note the router and vacuum in the corner. The dark circles on the letter faces are holes where lag bolts were driven in during the gluing operation. The holes are later filled with plugs, set flush to the letter-face surfaces.*

*Illus. 238. The author about to begin routing. A ¼-inch round-bottom bit will be used to out-line all letters, cutting only to a shallow depth.*

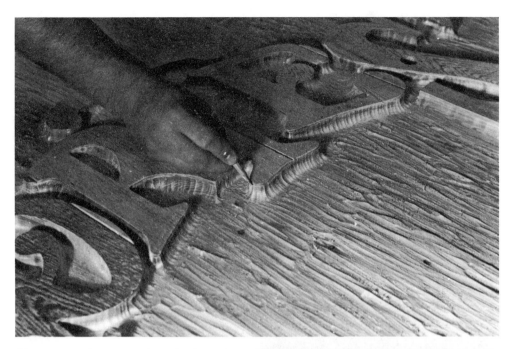

*Illus. 239 (above). A close look at the router-carved raised lettering. A 1-inch-diameter carbide round-nose bit was used to remove all of the background, cutting ⅞-inches deep. Routing was done with the grain, stopping the strokes right at the shallow-cut, outlined letters. Routing away the background consumed 72 hours alone.*

*Illus. 240 (right). A model (scaled at 1 inch to the foot) was made to check the right visual look for the post structure.*

*Illus. 241 (top left). The posts (made of 12-inch-square timbers) were cut, fitted, and hand-hewn, and brought to the construction site for final assembly. (See Illus. 18 on page 16 for the method of hand hewing.)*

*Illus. 242 (above). The post assembly is braced, lifted, and set into the holes with a forklift.*

*Illus. 243 (center left). The structure is leveled vertically and horizontally. The heavy equipment holds it plumb as the concrete sets in the holes.*

*Illus. 244 (bottom left). The forklift hauled the sign from the shop to the site and made easy work of hanging it on the post structure.*

# 10   Sandblasting Signs

According to *Signs of the Times* magazine, the cutting or etching of wood signs by sandblasting is nothing new. The magazine ran articles introducing some basic techniques in the 1930's. The process of impelling abrasive particles with a high-pressure air system actually originated in Great Britain in 1870. Today, because people are tiring of metal, plastic, and neon, the sandblasted signs are just starting to come into vogue. Modern equipment, easy-to-cut stencils, and the growing demand for unusual wood signs (large and small) provide the sandblasting sign-maker a new, easy, and growing medium in the field of wood signs. Sandblasted signs are beautiful, distinctive, and unique. They seem to be mysteriously made, causing people not in the "know" to ask, "How in the world do you do this?"

Essentially, this abrasive etching technique is the same process used to engrave names, art, and dates in granite and marble monuments—particularly tombstones. Engraving in wood is obviously easier and faster than sandblasting in stone and the wood craftsman has much more latitude for creative expression. The process is relatively easy to learn. In fact, it requires much less skill and practice to blast a professional-looking sign than it does to carve one by hand or to use a router freehand. Its ease was proven by our 17-year-old exchange student. She produced the name sign shown in Illustration 245 in her very first attempt. The process is basically this: (1) adhere the stencil, (2) transfer the design, (3) cut the stencil, and (4) blast.

The sandblast process can be used to make raised letters (Illus. 245 and 246), engraved work, or a combination of both (Illus. 247). Further dimensional effects can be achieved by combining hand-carved or router-shaped designs and borders with your sandblasted creations. Built-up borders, attached carvings, or ready-made ornaments can be fastened to the sign to produce dramatic, deep-dimensional signs of unparalleled appeal and individuality.

*Illus. 245. Sandblasting signs is easy, as exemplified by this one in flat-sawn redwood. It was made by 17-year-old Lis Kukla without any previous experience.*

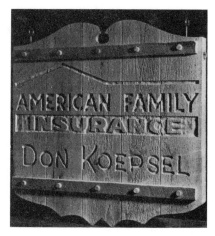

*Illus. 246 (above). A small sign in vertical-grained redwood.*

*Illus. 247 (right). This sign in rough-sawn cedar features engraved and raised sand-blasted lettering and freehand router work.*

**Woods for Sandblasting** include a wide variety of different species, but redwood is far superior to any other kind of wood in its desirable response to blasting. Cedar (the western red species) is next in line to redwood for "blastability" (Illus. 248). White cedar is considerably tougher than its "red brother," but it can be blasted well with heavy equipment and additional time (Illus. 247 and 249). Mahogany, walnut, spruce, and pine also respond well to blasting. Some woods, though apparently soft, do not blast easily. They seem to be too "spongy." Willow and butternut are good examples. Although I have blasted these, it takes

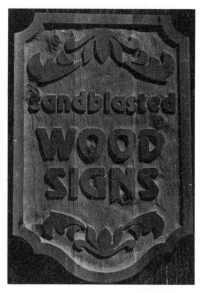

*Illus. 248 (above). A house number in flat-grained western red cedar.*

*Illus. 249 (right). Three boards of knotty flat-sawn cedar were glued edge to edge to make the width of this sign.*

102

three or four times longer than cedar or redwood and consumes a proportionate quantity of additional sand to get the job done.

Woods can be glued together, edge to edge, to make large panels. See Illustration 249 and refer to chapter 8. There may be some irregularity in depth along the glue lines due to varying hardness or grain patterns at the joint. If you select stock by carefully matching the kinds of wood and the face-grain patterns, you should achieve a uniformly blasted surface regardless of the glue line.

**Vertical Grain Versus Flat Grain** (Illus. 250) makes little difference to the "blastability" of the wood. However, each results in its own unique blast-textured surface qualities. Vertical-grain boards will have very pronounced, thin, straight lines as typified by the sign shown in Illustration 246. This effect is the result of the softer, less dense part of the tree's growth ring being blasted away faster than the harder areas. See Illustrations 245, 247, and 248, which show the texture of blasted surfaces resulting from boards having flat-grain faces. Remember that vertical-grain boards shrink and swell less than flat-sawn wood. They also do not warp as easily. On single-faced signs made from flat-grain boards, use the bark side of the board for the front as it will weather better than the pith side.

*Illus. 250. The type of grain pattern on the sign face is directly related to the kind of textured surface obtained from sandblasting.*

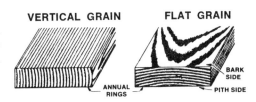

VERTICAL GRAIN    FLAT GRAIN

ANNUAL RINGS    BARK SIDE    PITH SIDE

**Knots** in all species of wood do not blast away easily and remain higher than the surrounding area. This may or may not be desirable, depending upon your personal preference. To some of us, knots are as much a natural part of wood as the sun is a part of daylight, and they should be a part of the overall plan. However, large knots overlapping the edges of letters will diminish the clarity and crispness of execution. Consequently, knots, if allowed, are best planned to end up in the background areas. If high knots are objectionable after initial blasting, cut them down with a chisel or router, and then blast the area again. Study Illustration 249.

**Equipment.** Your ability to blast various materials is related to the air-delivery of your air compressor and the matching suitability of your sandblaster unit. Test various materials for yourself to see which one gives you the depth you want in the shortest time. We've experimented with and tested many kinds of

*Illus. 251. An experiment with sandblasted particle board.*

materials—look at Illustration 251. Our unusual experiment in particle board proved to us that the potential for the sandblasting process has yet to be fully challenged.

The first step is to obtain the necessary equipment, or at least obtain the use of it. It's very expensive, and it would be foolish for the amateur to run out and buy the equipment without first gaining some experience and intelligent technical assistance. Check the Appendix for a list of sources you can write to for information about sandblasting equipment and related supplies. The essentials are: (1) an appropriate air compressor, (2) a sandblaster (also called a sandblast generator or "pot"), and (3) the masking material commonly referred to as sandblast stencil or tape.

If you can get on the good side of someone in the tombstone and monument business you will get a lot of help and information. Also check the yellow pages for sandblasting services, and talk to people in auto body repair and finishing shops where they use sandblasting to remove rust and old finishes. In fact, it would be a good idea to engage one of these services to blast your first sign — that is assuming you are not already equipped with some sort of compressor and sandblaster. If you look around hard enough and are somewhat lucky you may be able to purchase small quantities of the necessary supplies from one of the above businesses. Try your best to buy some stencil and adhesive from a monument carver. Otherwise, you can purchase through the sources listed at the end of the book. If all of your contacts fail, check out the equipment rental agencies in your city—many do rent portable compressors and sandblasters. With the appropriate equipment a small sign (10 inches by 24 inches) in redwood can be blasted in 15 to 20 minutes maximum. Consequently, it would be much more practical to take your first signs to someone with the equipment, rather than moving the equipment to your shop for only several minutes' work.

The equipment available for sandblasting today includes a wide range of sizes and optional features—all at various prices to satisfy your exact requirements and budget.

**Air Compressors** of the smaller sizes and capacities (often found in home workshops for occasional utility work) will not, as a rule, be satisfactory for you in the long run. If you have a compressor of the 1- to 1½-hp size, try it, but don't expect too much. Compressors of this size do not produce the quantity of continuous air delivery necessary for pleasurable blasting. As the horsepower on compressors increases, so does the amount of continuous air supply increase, and so does your delight in blasting. Compressors of 1½ hp will work, but you will soon be discouraged. Basically, compressor capacities are designated by horsepower (hp) and cfm (cubic feet per minute). Do not be misled by a compressor ad specifying a high psi (pounds per square inch). When you set the compressor to increase the psi, the cfm capacity becomes less. For example, a typical 3-hp compressor has a 6.9 cfm rating at 40 psi but drops to a 5.8 cfm when the pressure is increased to 90 psi.

You will find that most businesses using air to either lift a garage hoist, sandblast car bodies, or operate air tools will have at least a 5-hp compressor. Sandblasting wood signs (with redwood as the standard) can be done satisfactorily with a 3-hp unit, easily with a 5-hp unit, and very quickly with the 7½- to 10-hp units that the professionals insist upon. Thus, the rate or speed at which you can blast or etch away wood varies directly with the species of wood and amount of air supply—but most directly with the latter. Our compressor is a 7½-hp unit with a 24.6 cfm rating at 175 psi. This is more than adequate. A 5-hp unit with an air delivery of 15 to 18 cfm at 175 psi would be ideal for most serious-minded wood-blasting craftsmen. Remember, high psi is not a major factor in sandblasting—you will get good results with 35 to 80 psi as greater pressures are seldom required. Continuous air supply is most important. The air requirements are also dictated by the kind of sandblasting unit and the size of the nozzle opening.

**The Sandblaster** (Illus. 252–254) can be purchased from the economy (limited service) line to the high production machine. As a rule, sandblasters are designated by required cfm of air in accordance with recommended hose sizes and nozzle diameters. Many optional features are available, and some are superfluous for occasional use while others are almost a necessity for a full-time operation. Professionals like larger sand-holding capacities so they do not have to shut down to load sand. However, this is not usually a major inconvenience with an average size 150-pound pot. Sandblasters function in several basic ways. They all have a pot which holds the sand and various levers and valves to control the mixture of sand and air. Sandblasters can be categorized as either suction-feed or pressure-

*Illus. 252 (left). An economy, suction-feed sandblaster. Illus. 253 (center). A medium-duty sandblaster with wheels for portability, This unit holds 100 pounds of sand and requires 10 cfm at 80 psi with a ³/₃₂-inch-diameter nozzle bore. Illus. 254 (right). A pressure-type sandblaster features a water extractor and sand-control lever. Note the ceramic nozzle resting on the filling screen.*

feed units. Suction- (or siphon-) feed units can operate on as little as 4 to 7 cfm of air.

The better blasters are the pressurized type, and they usually require at least a 5-hp compressor around the 25-cfm range. This kind of unit allows the use of a ⅛-inch-diameter nozzle opening and will consume approximately 100 pounds of sand per hour. Changing the nozzle size changes the cfm requirement. A smaller nozzle, such as ³/₃₂ inch, requires about 11 cfm at 70 psi or 12 cfm at 80 psi. Unless you have ample space, or can afford a special indoor room or booth, you will likely be forced to do your blasting outside. It is imperative that your compressor be located (piped) a safe distance away from the blasting area so the compressor's intake air is not contaminated with sand or dust particles. One desirable, highly recommended feature is a water extractor which will eliminate many problems related to clogged valves, nozzles, and sand passages. There is always moisture in compressed air.

Nozzles for the sandblaster are made of materials that resist the abrasive nature of the moving sand. Tungsten carbide, boron carbide, and ceramic are good nozzle materials, with ceramic the most economical. Ceramic outwears cheaper cast-iron and steel nozzles.

Only your own experience, coupled with sound technical advice for your specific needs, will determine the best equipment for you.

**Abrasives and Blasting Media** can include any granular material that will go through the filling screen of the blaster. Some cut faster, others have polishing effects. Dry beach sand, silica sand, glass beads, metal shot, garnet, silicon carbide, and aluminum oxide are typically used. The most expensive are silicon carbide and aluminum oxide. They are the hardest and fastest cutting abrasives, but they also accelerate wear to nozzles and other parts of the blaster. Silica sand is available at most building centers and lumberyards. It costs about $3.00 to $3.50 per 100-pound bag, which can do six to ten small redwood name signs. Blasting abrasives are classified by a nominal mesh size (U.S. Sieve). Generally, the coarser the grit, the faster the cutting action. For most sign work, 40 to 80 grit is suitable. One hundred grit and finer is not recommended. Use the 40 grit for fast cutting on large signs where delicate detail is not so essential. Use 60 grit for the majority of your work on small signs.

*Caution*: Be sure to use suitable operator safety and protective accessories. Always wear a dust filter (respirator) covering mouth and nose. Prolonged breathing of dust may cause delayed lung injury (silicosis). A blasting hood (helmet) is also a must item for protection against rebounding abrasives. An inexpensive canvas hood with a viewing window and ventilation screens can be used for outdoor work. Outdoor blasting in large opened cardboard shipping boxes, plastic covered crates, or similar improvised booths will allow you to reclaim some of the sand for reuse.

**Stencil Materials for Sandblasting** wood signs (Illus. 255) have in the past been essentially a soft rubber sheet material approximately $^3/_{32}$ to $^1/_8$ inch thick with a rubber-based adhesive backing designed especially for the marble and granite monument industry. Today, three companies provide sandblasting stencil material: Anchor Continental, Inc.; Custom Coated Products Co., Div. of Doyco

*Illus. 255. A roll of sandblast stencil. All have an easy-to-remove liner that exposes the adhesive-coated backing.*

Corp.; and the 3-M Company. The major problem with these materials is that they are designed especially for the monument carver, not for wood sign sandblasting. They can be made to work, but their adhesives are formulated to adhere to the smoothly polished surfaces of marble and granite. The stencil produced by Custom Coated Products Company is a new vinyl-based material, whereas the other companies produce a rubber-based stencil. Blasting in stone obviously requires a heavier-gauge stencil material than is needed for redwood.

Indications are that thinner and less expensive stencil materials designed especially for wood sign work will become available in the near future. This eventuality will come sooner as companies receive more and more requests for stencil materials designed for wood sign fabricators. The primary requirement for using the stencils available today is that they adhere well to the wood surface and remain tightly secured throughout the blasting operation.

The most popular stencils used by wood sign blasters are Anchor No. 111 "easy cut," 3-M 508 Gen. Purpose and 507 "Buttercut," and Custom Coated Products No. 100 vinyl Gold Seal. Most come in rolls of 10-yard lengths with a width of 30 inches or more, but narrower sizes as small as 10½ inches are available from at least one company. Small pieces can be butted tightly together to make full use of your scrap materials.

**Adhering the Stencil** to the wood. To blast successfully, the stencil must not come loose or lift up during blasting. Don't rely on the pressure-sensitive adhesive on the back of the stencil. The bond between the wood and the stencil can be improved by using some type of contact cement. Anchor and 3-M provide contact cements for use on non-polished surfaces, which also hold well on rough and/or prefinished wood. These are solvent based. Vinyl stencils can be applied with

*Illus. 256 (left). A sign blank prefinished with clear varnish. Note the knotty, flat-cut boards glued together.*

*Illus. 257 (below). Rolling the stencil gives the necessary pressure to assure a good bond.*

*Illus. 258. Trimming off the excess stencil. Here the sign is pressed down against several layers of newspaper as the excess stencil is cut away.*

water adhesives. The easiest procedure is to completely finish the face of the sign (Illus. 256) with a suitable varnish or pigmented enamel before applying the stencil. This procedure enables you to remove the stencil and the remaining contact cement easily after blasting. However, we don't like clear surface finishes, such as varnish, for exterior signs because we know these finishes don't last. Thus, for exterior signs start with the raw unfinished wood—either rough-sawn or smoothly sanded, depending upon the desired results.

Cut the stencil about an inch or so larger than the sign blank. Remember you can butt small pieces of stencil together to cover large areas. Just be sure no gaps are left in the joints. The key to making the stencil adhere is to apply contact cement (liquid brush-on or the spray type such as 3-M's Aerosol No. 77) to both the wood and the adhesive side (backing) of the stencil. Roll the stencil down (Illus. 257), applying pressure as you would in applying a plastic laminate material to a counter top. Puncture any small air bubbles that might appear. This pressure step drives the adhesive into the pores of the wood, making a good bond. However, cement in the pores of smooth wood or in the cavities of rough-sawn wood could cause problems during subsequent staining or finishing. On rough-sawn wood, the cement remaining after stencil removal can be removed with a light dusting from the sandblaster. Signs that will have smooth, unblasted areas can be cleaned up by carefully hand sanding to remove the cement left in the unblasted surfaces. Once the stencil is glued down, the overhang can be left as is or trimmed back to the edges of the sign as desired. See Illustrations 258–260. Transferring the pattern and layout is usually easier with the stencil trimmed to the edges.

We usually lay out our patterns on heavy paper and transfer the design to the stencil with carbon paper. The stencil layout is cut with a sharply pointed knife such as shown in Illustration 261. This skill will take a little practice. You must

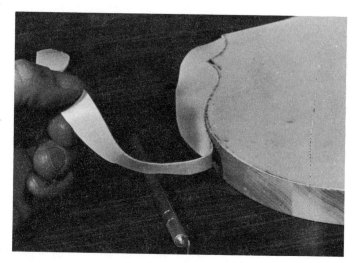

Illus. 259. The excess stencil is removed from the contoured edges of the sign blank prior to layout and blasting.

cut completely through the stencil in one pass, but do not allow the point to cut too deeply. If you cut too deeply and go into the wood, the knife will tend to follow the grain of the wood rather than allowing you to make smooth-flowing curves. Use a plastic triangle or steel straightedge as a guide for cutting all the straight lines. Be sure that all lines have been cut. Peel the stencil off, exposing only those areas that are to be sandblasted (Illus. 262). *Caution*: Peel the stencil very carefully and pull at low angle *with* the grain (Illus. 263) so that the stencil doesn't pull up large slivers of wood. After the cutting is completed and all of the stencil removed, press the stencil down with the roller once more to make sure all areas are bonded well.

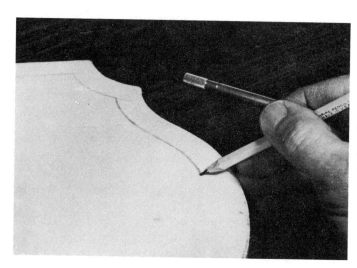

Illus. 260. A line for a border is finger-gauged along the contoured edge.

*Illus. 261.*
*Cutting the stencil. The*
*knife is held vertically*
*so no undercuts are*
*made.*

*Illus. 262.*
*Stencil has been par-*
*tially removed, expos-*
*ing wood areas for*
*blasting. This job will*
*be blasted to two levels*
*of depth. The exposed*
*area will be blasted*
*first. The trees will be*
*unmasked later and*
*blasted to a shallower*
*depth.*

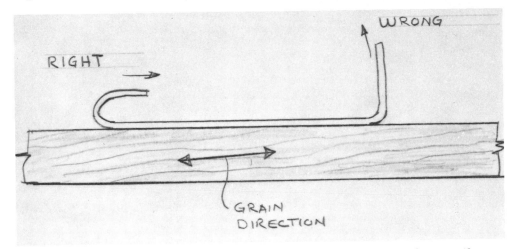

*Illus. 263. Use a peeling motion, going with the grain, to remove the stencil.*

*Illus. 264. Here the stencil is cut and ready for blasting. Only about one-third of the area of this sign is to be blasted, so scrap pieces of hardboard or plywood were used to make a protective sheathing over the areas not covered with the rubber stencil.*

When only part of a sign is to be blasted, there is no point to covering the entire sign face with the rubber stencil, which is expensive. Old pieces of plywood or hardboard can be used as a protective sheathing overlapping the rubber stencil (Illus. 264).

**Blasting a Sign.** Load your blaster (Illus. 265), screening the abrasive into the pot. Turn on the compressor. Set your pressure to match the nozzle size. Prop your sign blank up so you can blast in a comfortable standing position. I use an old sawbuck (Illus. 264) for a blasting bench. Put on your safety gear (Illus. 266) and turn on the air at the sandblaster. With blasters having a mixture control, gradually discharge the sand from the nozzle. It is important to have the right

*Illus. 265 (left). Loading the pot and screening silica sand. Illus. 266 (right). Getting ready to blast. A lever starts and stops the abrasive stream. Note the protective helmet.*

*Illus. 267. The first step completed for blasting to two depths. Now the stencil will be removed from around the letters, and the trees will be blasted — but they will still be raised above the background area.*

sand adjustment. This has been achieved when a blue-colored-flamelike blast emits from the nozzle. Excessive sand retards cutting efficiency and too little sand wastes time, energy, and air.

The best results will be achieved by holding the nozzle at a right angle to the work and about 6 to 12 inches away. Move the nozzle in a continuous, small circular motion over the entire surface until the desired depth is achieved. We usually like to cut to at least ½ inch in depth, somewhat less on smaller signs (Illus. 267). If the heat generated at the blast area appears to burn the stencil material, drop the air pressure. Keep experimenting until you have the right combination of air pressure adjustment, nozzle size, sand flow efficiency, and optimum cutting time.

Once you have completed the blasting to your satisfaction, don't be too eager to remove the stencil. You may want to stain the background at this point or spray it with an aerosol, using the stencil as your paint masking. When you do remove the rubber stencil, lift it carefully, pulling at a low angle with the grain (Illus. 263).

One of the disadvantages of the sandblasting process is that the stencil cannot be reused once it has been removed. This is usually of minor concern because the end results are so overwhelmingly satisfactory. However, we have made reusable pre-cut letters and numbers (Illus. 268) with moderate success. Simply find a thin, rigid, easily cut material such as sheet polystyrene. Apply the stencil to one surface and cut the rubber and the plastic simultaneously with a shears or scroll saw. Test various contact cements until you find one that provides a suitable bond

*Illus. 268 (left). These reusable pre-cut stencils were made by applying regular sandblast stencils onto polystyrene plastic. Illus. 269 (right). This house number was sandblasted with reusable stencils.*

that will hold up throughout the blast (Illus. 269).

Some examples showing easy-to-execute name signs are given in Illustrations 270–272. Other examples showing the adaptability of sandblasting to delicate details are shown in Illustration 273. Two examples of large commercial signs are presented in Illustrations 274 and 275.

*Illus. 270–272. Some examples of small, sandblasted name signs.*

Illus. 273. This sign shows the fine detail that can be achieved by sandblasting.

Illus. 274 and 275. Large sandblasted signs. Sign at bottom has a built-up frame for extra depth. (Both signs designed and crafted by Jason Morgan.)

# 11 Finishing Signs

Woodworkers who get involved in making wood signs are usually experienced in all areas of woodcrafting and already have a good background of knowledge about wood finishing.There are a great many good reference books available that cover every aspect of wood finishing. This chapter will include only a few suggested techniques and some philosophical ideas for your consideration. Finishing wood signs is not particularly different from finishing other wood products specifically for indoor or outdoor use.

The primary reasons for finishing your sign include: (1) to improve the beauty or appearance, (2) to improve its legibility, (3) to protect it from dirt or stain, and (4) to slow down deterioration caused by weathering. With these points in mind, determine if you really want to finish the sign at all. Sometimes, in certain settings, because of the depth and shadows cast on deeply cut dimensional signs, they have just the right subtle contrast to make the sign readable but not shocking. Signs left unfinished must truly rely on the "raw" emphasis of their natural wood features (Illus. 276).

However, most people expect a finish on their sign because they are accustomed to having their wood products finished. Since wood is a natural, organic material it seems somewhat hypocritical to cover its best inherent features with pigmented finishes—particularly paint. Paint, in addition to its preservative qualities, is intended to cover or hide wood. It's our opinion that, whenever possible, the natural qualities of wood should be emphasized, not hidden. If the sign must be finished, we recommend clear, natural, non-pigment, non-glossy finishes for indoor signs. Essentially the same is recommended for outdoor

*Illus. 276. A rustic sign is rasped to give the edge a worn, weathered look. Would finishing really make this sign look better?*

*Illus. 277. Remove rough fibres with fine sandpaper.*

signs, but the problems associated with moisture and the sun's rays must be contended with—either by directly challenging the eventual weathering problems or simply cooperating with them to remain in harmony with nature. (More about weathering later.)

This is not to say that one shouldn't paint a wood sign. If, in your opinion, paint improves the sign, paint it. Certainly paint (or any pigmented finish) adds color and emphasis, increases interest, and draws attention. Paints can be used selectively to complement the natural features of wood rather than hide them totally. When possible, select soft, "earthy" colors for backgrounds, with contrasts of darker or brighter hues for lettering and other design features needing emphasis. A wood sign that has a bright-red painted background contrasted with fluorescent yellow or gloss white is just too close to the "plastic look." A soft, light tan background, for example, with black or a dull, flat, non-glossy white lettering has good contrast, too. It's readable but not shocking or irritating—this kind of combination is more in line with the natural, environmentally pleasing appearance for which wood signs are preferred in the first place. The point we are attempting to make is this: give very careful thought and planning to your choice of finish. A perfect, artistically created sign, often involving hours of labor and tender loving care, can be ruined and cheapened quickly with just a few brush strokes.

**Preparation.** Even your most rustic types of signs should give the appearance of skill and good craftsmanship in their execution. Be sure to sand off rough fibres (hairs) that will obstruct the appearance or that will interfere with your painting or finishing work (Illus. 277). If the sign is to receive a clear or natural finish, be sure to remove all pencil marks that might show through the

117

*Illus. 278 (above). Remove all pencil marks. An eraser works for rough-sawn stock and sandpaper works for smooth surfaces.*

*Illus. 279 (right). This effect was achieved by thoroughly charring the sign with a propane torch.*

finish (Illus. 278). If the surfaces are intended to be smooth, then fill holes and other imperfections and follow with a careful, thorough sanding. Rustic signs allow more latitude since the visibility of tool marks, dents, etc., often does more to add to the appearance than detract from it — it adds character and authenticity.

**Finishing Interior Signs.** Indoor signs do not need protection from moisture and the sun's rays, but they generally require higher standards of appearance and finishing craftsmanship. This is because the viewer is usually closer to interior signs. Almost any kind of finish can be used on indoor signs. Use penetrating Danish oils, varnishes, or lacquers for clear, natural finishes. Any of the various kinds of wood stains available today can be used to improve the color or emphasize the grain. Use exterior stains if they give you the "touch" or color you want. Most exterior stains are easier to use. Letters, borders, and art work can be colored with any type of pigmented colors in latex, acrylics, watercolors, paints, or enamels.

One idea for doing a job quickly is to use soft-tip markers to color in routed or carved letters and borders, or to color the upper surfaces of raised letters and similar surfaces, such as details of carvings. Leave the backgrounds natural.

Then finish the job off quickly, using a clear aerosol spray that dries quickly. Thus, the job is done quickly and inexpensively without mess or cleanup.

Today, you see a lot of wooden items that are randomly burned or slightly charred with a propane or blow torch. This technique can be equally effective on wood signs—particularly the rustic types. It is a good idea to experiment on some scrap to achieve the right technique for the desired effect. Excessive charring can be removed with a bristle brush or steel wool. These burned or charred surfaces should be covered or sealed with a clear aerosol spray finish.

Illustration 279 shows a sign with router-cut raised letters. It was not sanded or sandblasted, nor was any liquid finish applied to it. The surfaces were thoroughly charred with a propane torch, burning away the softer areas of the wood grain and also rounding off sharply cut corners. It was then brushed vigorously with a bristle brush, like a shoe-shining brush, to remove the charred ash. Western red and white cedars, Douglas fir, spruce, and redwood work well with this technique. If this sign were left outdoors in the sun, it would eventually bleach out. For some, this might also create a very desirable effect.

Another "quickie" technique, often employed by professionals who rout signs at fairs and amusement parks, is to use fast-drying spray paint. They spray,

*Illus. 280 (top left). To paint routed letters quickly, use spray paint.*

*Illus. 281 (top right). Clean off the surface, leaving only the painted letters.*

*Illus. 282 (bottom right). A hand plane, jointer or belt sander can also be used.*

covering the sign completely and usually the edges as well (Illus. 280). After the paint dries, they remove the extra paint from the surface with a belt sander, rasp (Illus. 281), or hand plane (Illus. 282), leaving only the lettering and edges painted. Leaving about 10 percent of the paint remaining on the surface adds interest. This technique is especially effective if a rough-sawn board was used initially (Illus. 283). The project is usually finished with a quick-drying aerosol spray. This technique can also be employed to finish exterior signs, provided an exterior paint is used. However, it is recommended that the last step of applying the clear spray finish be eliminated, as these finishes do not weather well at all.

**Finishing Exterior Signs.** Basically, your finishing choices are: (1) none at all, (2) natural, (3) stains, (4) paints, or (5) a combination of any of the above. As mentioned previously, the finishing of exterior wood signs must take into account the forces of nature that tend to deteriorate wood and many finishes. The simplest approach is not to finish at all, but to cooperate with nature and allow the raw wood to weather (Illus. 284). This appearance is often preferred anyway since the weathered look is delightfully rustic. Some minor cracking and checking is to be expected, but other wear and tear is minimal at best. Experts say that exposed unfinished wood will wear away at a rate of only about ¼ inch every 100 years.

**Weathering.** Nearly all unfinished woods will eventually turn to a beautiful silvery grey (Illus. 284). Although the first color changes seem to indicate that this is not true, it is true. The naturally colored darker woods will at first become lighter, and lighter ones will at first become darker. This is because some of the extractives (chemicals) in the wood come to the surface. But in due time the surface will turn silvery grey as it continues to be exposed to sun and moisture. According to the California Redwood Association, this change may be quickened in redwood by wetting the wood with a fine mist from a garden hose.

*Illus. 283. Leaving paint on some of the surface area adds a little interest.*

*Illus. 284. This cedar sign has been left unfinished (except for the lettering) and allowed to weather naturally.*

The rate at which wood naturally reaches the optimum weathered silvery grey will vary among different kinds of woods, and depend also upon the amount of exposure to direct sunlight and moisture. Sometimes the change may only take several months, but if the sign is facing to the north or is shaded by an overhang the total change may take a very long time, or the sign may never become uniformly weathered. For this reason, we try to avoid signs with little protective roofs over them. These roofs usually shade and protect only the upper part of the sign. The lower areas still receive sun exposure and rain. The eventual consequence is a sign face that is not uniformly weathered.

**Natural Exterior Finishes.** At first, you might assume that a good exterior "spar" varnish is all that is required to protect your handiwork and keep its natural look well preserved under the varnish's transparent film. However, both the California Redwood Association and The Forest Products Laboratory do not recommend clear film-forming finishes, such as varnish or other synthetic resins, for long-term outdoor use. After considerable testing, they have concluded that these finishes, within a year, will turn a distasteful yellow, and will crack and peel. The only way to rectify this condition is through complete removal and total refinishing. Various penetrating oils are also not recommended for exterior finishes since they are susceptible to mildew. The two best solutions recommended for exterior finishes are water-repellent preservatives and bleaching agents.

**Water-Repellent Preservatives** will modify the natural weathering of wood. This solution is sold under trade names such as "Woodlife," "Pentaseal," "Wood Tox," and a number of others. These water repellents are very easy to apply and

*Illus. 285 (left). This sign was finished entirely with water-repellent preservative (only lettering is painted for contrast) to retard weathering. Illus. 286 (right). Bleaching oils speed up natural weathering (by chemical reaction) and are one-coat, lifelong finishes.*

they penetrate deeply into the wood. No need to worry about lap marks, brush strokes, or runs, because they don't show. Water repellents retard the growth of fungi (mildew), keep water staining at the ends of boards to a minimum, reduce warping, and also protect woods that have a low resistance to decay. This preservative solution can be easily applied by dipping or brushing. All edges and ends of boards should be liberally treated. Rough-sawn stock will absorb more finish than smooth surfaces, and thus the treatment will be more durable. The best application for durability and performance is achieved by repeated applications to the "point of refusal." A clear, golden tan color can be achieved on rough-sawn cedar and redwood, and the weathering problems will be greatly slowed. Eventually, with exposure to sun and rain, the wood will slowly turn to a driftwood grey. Water repellents also make an excellent base coat for other finishes. Consequently, the entire sign can be treated first. Then, letters and other designs, borders, and so on can be painted as desired. See Illustration 285. Water repellents contain toxic chemicals, so be sure to heed the warnings on the manufacturer's label.

**Bleaching Oils or Bleaching Stains** very effectively speed and advance, by chemical action, the weathered appearance. Most also contain some grey pigment which eliminates the early darkening in weathering. Bleaching solutions give an instant grey look, providing a uniform appearance during the time it takes the chemical to react with the wood and effect the color change. Bleaching produces a maintenance-free finish (Illus. 286). Because of the pigment, avoid leaving telltale brush-mark overlaps and runs during application. Usually only one coat is necessary because the color it produces lasts as long as the wood itself. It is not a film-forming finish and therefore will never blister or peel even if excessive moisture enters the wood. Inexpensively priced, bleaching solutions are available from most local paint stores and lumber dealers.

**Pigmented Semi-Transparent Stains** provide color but do not hide the natural characteristics of the wood. They penetrate deeply, do not form a film on the surface of the wood, and they allow most of the grain to show through. These stains do not peel or blister, even when moisture may enter the wood. Penetrating semi-transparent stains can be used on smooth surfaces, but they will last longer on rough-sawn textured signs (Illus. 287). Up to 10 years service on rough-sawn

*Illus. 287 (left). This sign background of rough-sawn cedar with semitransparent stain has a carefree finish service-life of 10 or more years.*

*Illus. 288 (below). Applying pigmented penetrating stains to backgrounds is easy.*

*Illus. 289. Opaque stain was used to finish the rough-sawn textured background of this sign.*

surfaces can be expected with two coats. The second coat should be applied before the first one dries so that both coats penetrate. These stains are very easy to apply (Illus. 288), but care must be taken to avoid lap marks. There are many, many colors available (including some excellent natural wood tones) from your local paint dealer. Ask him for sample color "chips" to help make color selections. One company provides stains on "chips" of several different species of wood (including pine, cedar, and redwood) that are smooth on one side and rough-textured on the other.

*Illus. 290 (above). To obtain the greatest degree of durability, raised letter-surfaces should be primed before painting. Illus. 291 (right). Routed lettering must be carefully painted by hand.*

**Opaque Stains** are more like paint because they have film-forming characteristics. These are especially good on rough-sawn backgrounds, where they last about twice as long as on smooth wood surfaces. Rough-sawn surfaces for signs are highly recommended because, even with heavily pigmented stains, more of the wood texture shows (Illus. 289). Opaque stains (also called solid-color stains) are preferred over paints or enamels because they are flat or dull in appearance rather than glossy. Usually only one coat is required and primers are not necessary. Opaque exterior stains are available locally.

**Paints and Enamels** of any serviceable exterior type can be used for coloring in letters and other details. Paints retard moisture penetration. Painted surfaces offer the best protection when achieved by this three-step procedure: (1) treat with water-repellent preservative, (2) apply primer (Illus. 290), and (3) apply two coats of latex, alkyd, or oil-base house paint.

**Coloring Routed Lettering** with paints, solid-color stains, or exterior enamels can be done by careful application with artist's brushes (Illus. 291). A sharp line should exist where the surface of the letter meets the background surface of the sign. Another system that shows much promise is pour-in epoxy for signs with flat-bottomed, engraved lettering. It is best applied to raw, unfinished wood. Epoxy resins suitable for exterior use do the job quickly and easily when measured, pigment added (about 1 teaspoon per cup of resin), mixed, and simply poured in (Illus. 292). Simply pour a "bead" onto the approximate center area of each letter. The resin tends to flow out to the edges and will self-level. See

*Illus. 292. With the container crimped to form a pouring spout, the pigmented epoxy is poured onto the routed letter-surfaces.*

*Illus. 293. A small stick is used to spread the resin toward the uncovered areas of each letter.*

Illustrations 293 and 294. The sign must remain level and should be covered with some sort of dust shield until the resin cures. One disadvantage of this technique is that letters that are not cut cleanly may have an ink-blotter effect around rough fibres, in which case the resin is pulled somewhat beyond the containing edge of the letter and into the background. When you stain the background later, any excess that may drip or run onto the cured epoxy lettering can be wiped off easily with a rag.

**Cutout Letters** are often colored with transparent or opaque, solid-color stains before they are attached to their appropriate backgrounds. See Illustrations 295

*Illus. 294. The flow-coated resin in the letters will self-level to a very smooth finish and will be permanently welded to the wood.*

*Illus. 295. A painted letter, with the routed edge highlighted for interest and contrast.*

*Illus. 296 (left). Cutout letters finished with transparent stain. Highlighted routed edges are solid color.*

*Illus. 297 (right). These posts are getting the last coat of preservative just before they are set into the ground.*

and 296. Always finish all surfaces, when possible, for resistance to moisture and for balance to reduce warping tendencies.

**Reflective Sheeting and Paints** are sometimes appropriately applied to sign lettering. Various materials in many colors are available to allow nighttime reading when viewed by reflected light. Flexible, reflective sheeting with an adhesive-coated backing makes application easy onto most clean, dry, and smooth surfaces. It generally has a life range of five to six years. Liquid reflective coatings, available in a limited number of colors, are applied like paint and last from four to seven years without recoating. The paint-on coatings are unobtrusive during daytime viewing, as they have a textured satin finish. Materials of this type are available at paint and household hardware stores locally, or through the suppliers listed in the Appendix.

**Preservative Treatment for Posts** (Illus. 297), when necessary, should be done at the most opportune time—preferably before other finishes have been applied to the in-ground areas of the post. Several coats are best and these can often be applied simultaneously with other finish coats. Give the posts a heavy, generous coat just prior to installation. Refer to page 13 for information about post materials that do not need any brush-on preservatives.

# Alphabets

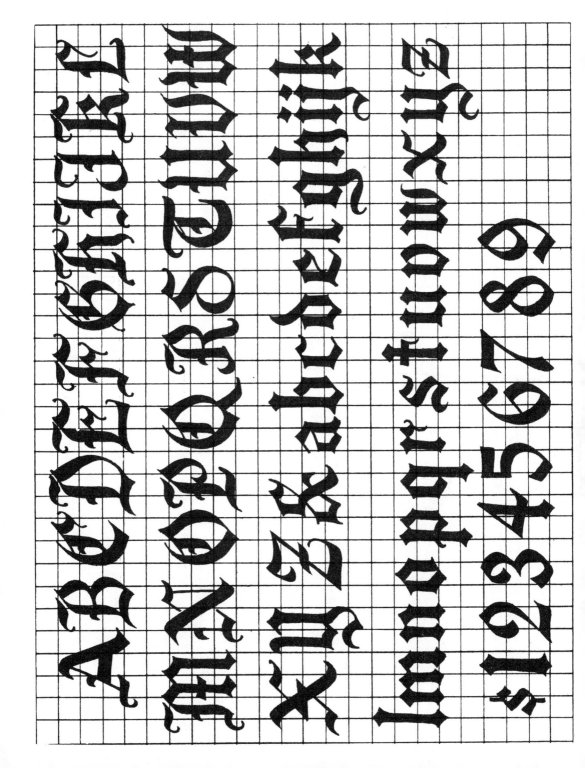

# Appendix
# Sources of Supplies

## DISTRIBUTORS OF SUPPLIES AND EQUIPMENT

### Alphabet Patterns, Templates (Die-Cuts)

Abbeon Cal., Inc.
Albert Constantine & Son, Inc.
Craftplans
Display Craft, Inc.
Hallcraft Products Co.
Walter Hartlauer
Harwell's Enterprises
Integrated Laser System, Inc.
K C Graphics
Manhattan Wood Systems, Inc.
Mastercraft Plans
Mutual Plans
Mutual Aids
Paulow Industries
The Woodworkers Store
A. Van Wormer

### Rub-On Dry-Transfer Letters

Chartpak
Graphic Products Corp.
Hearlihy & Co.
K C Graphics
Letraset USA, Inc.
Pressure Graphics
Southern Sign Supply
Triarco Arts & Crafts
Zipatone, Inc.

### Vinyl Letters

W. H. Brady Co.
Demco Educational Corp.
Die-Kuts, Inc.
Johnson Plastics
K C Graphics
Kinduell Screen Products, Inc.
Letter Rite, Inc.
Sav-Sets
Triarco Arts & Crafts
Zipatone, Inc.

### Hand Tools (Clamps, Chisels, Boring Tools, Etc.)

Brookstone Co.
Albert Constantine & Son, Inc.
Craftsman Wood Service Co.
The Craftool Co.
Dremel Mfg.
Frog Tool Co.
John Harra Wood & Supply Co.
Leichtung, Inc.
Sears Roebuck & Co.
The Upholstery Supply Co.
Garrett Wade Co.
Woodcarvers Supply Co.
Woodcraft Supply Corp.
The Woodworkers' Store

## Enlarging Projectors (Opaque and Overhead)

Advance Office Systems
Art-O-Graph, Inc.
Bell & Howell Co., Audio Visual Products Div.
Charles Beseler Co.
Buhl, Inc.
Buhl Optical
Demco Educational Corp.
Demolux, Inc.
Elmo Mfg. Corp.
Hoppman Corp.
Johnson Plastics
K C Graphics
Kalart Victor Corp.
Projection Optics Co., Inc.
Rigyt Damar, Div. Potts Optics & Mfg. Co.
Cecil E. Sanders Co.
George R. Snell Associates, Inc.
Southern Sign Supply
Squibb-Taylor Inc.
Standard Projector & Equipt. Co.
Testrite Instrument Co., Inc.
Visionvue Instruments
Wensco Sign Supplies
Weiser — Robodyne Corp.

## Wood Slabs

American Handicrafts Stores
Craftsman Wood Service
Weird Wood

## Wood Ornaments and Mouldings

Bendix Mouldings, Inc.
Albert Constantine & Son, Inc.
Craftsman Wood Service
The Woodworkers' Store

## Transparency-Making Equipment and Supplies

Lany Fax of America, Inc.
3-M Company, Visual Products Div.

## Router Bits

A-1 Carbide
Anthe Machine Works
Bimex, Inc.
Craftsman Wood Service Co.
Deluxe Saw & Tool Co.
Dremel Mfg.
Ekstrom, Carlson & Co.
Frog Tool Co.
Her-Saf Products
Lineberry Foundry & Machine Co.
Luxite Corp.
Millers Falls Power Tools
North American Products Corp.
Garland Engineering & Mfg. Co.
Onsrud Cutter Mfg. Co.
Rockwell Power Tool
Charles G.G. Schmidt & Co.
Sears Roebuck & Co.
Stanley Industrial Power Tools
The Upholstery Supply Co.
Wisconsin Knife Works

## Router Bit Sharpening and Grinding Services

A-1 Carbide
Anthe Machine Works
Bimex, Inc.
Ekstrom, Carlson & Co.
John Harra Wood & Supply Co.
North American Products Corp.
Onsrud Cutter Mfg. Co.
Virginia Machine Tool Co.
Wisconsin Knife Works

## Exterior Glues

Frog Tool Co.
Geougeon Brothers, Inc.
Wilhold Glues
Woodcraft Supply

## Letter Adhesives

Southern Sign Supply
Universal Adhesives

## Reflective (Liquids, Sheeting—Fluorescents)

Chromatic Paint Corp.
Southern Sign Supply
3-M Company
Wensco Sign Supplies

## Gold Leaf (Kits and Materials)

K C Graphics
W. H. Kemp Div., Absolute
   Coatings, Inc.
Kurz-Hastings, Inc.
School Products Co., Inc.
Southern Sign Supply
Wensco Sign Supplies

## Miscellaneous Sign Hardware

Edward W. Daniel Co.
Southern Sign Supply
Universal Metal Chain Co., Inc.

## Sandblast Stencil (Tape)

Anchor Continental, Inc.
Custom Coated Products,
   Div. Dayco Corp.
3-M Company, Industrial Tape Div.

## Sandblasting Equipment and Supplies

A.L.C. Co., Inc.
Abrading Machinery and Supply Co
Binks Mfg. Co.
Blast-It-All, Inc.
Cleveland Metal Abrasive Co.
Exolon Company
Hunter Associates
P. K. Lindsay Co., Inc.
Micro-Beads Inc.
Northeast Power Products, Inc.
Ottawa Silica Co.
George Pfaff, Inc.
Ruemelin Mfg. Co.
Titan Abrasive Systems, Inc.

## Paints and Finishes

Consumers Paint Factory, Inc.
Danacolors, Inc.
Geougeon Brothers, Inc.
K C Graphics
W. H. Kemp Div., Absolute
   Coatings, Inc.
Cecil E. Sanders Co.
Southern Sign Supply
3-M Company

## Brushes

K C Graphics
Cecil E. Sanders Co.
Southern Sign Supply
Triarco Arts & Crafts
Wensco Sign Supplies

## Pre-Cut Portrait Sandblast Stencils

Classic Images, Inc.

## Sign Carving and Routing Machines

Walter Hartlauer Co.
Kimball Woodcarver Co.
Kurt Manufacturing Co.
Laskowski Enterprises, Inc.
Marlin Industries
Quality Industries, Inc.
Sears Roebuck & Co.
Wood Graphics Co.

## Stencil Knives

Griffin Mfg. Co., Inc.
K C Graphics
Southern Sign Supply

## Safety Products (Respirators, Etc.)

Binks Mfg. Co.
General Scientific Equip. Co.
Industrial Safety & Security Co.
Woodcraft Supply Corp.

## Wood Mailboxes and Kits

Spielmans Wood Works

## Pounce Wheels

Griffin Mfg. Co., Inc.
K C Graphics
Southern Sign Supply

# ADDRESSES OF COMPANIES AND SUPPLIERS

A.L.C. Co., Inc.
P.O. Box 506
Medina, OH 44256

A-1 Carbide
10637 Midway Ave.
Cerritos, CA 90701

Abbeon Cal Inc.
123-305F Gray Ave.
Santa Barbara, CA 93101

Abrading Machinery and Supply Co.
2340 West Wabansia Ave.
Chicago, IL 60647

The Advance Products Co., Inc.
P.O. Box 2178 Central at Wabash
Wichita, KS 67214

American Handicrafts
Box 791
Fort Worth, TX 76101

Anchor Continental, Inc.
200 So. Beltline Boulevard
Columbus, SC 29250

Anthe Machine Works
407 Madison Ave.
Covington, KY 41011

Artograph, Inc.
529 So. 7th St.
Minneapolis, MN 55415

Bell & Howell Co.
Audio Visual Products Div.
7100 McCormick Rd.
Chicago, IL 60645

Bendix Mouldings, Inc.
235 Pegasus Ave.
Northvale, NJ 07647

Charles Beseler, Co.
8 Fernwood Rd.
Florham Park, NJ 07932

Bimex, Inc.
487 Armor Circle NE
Atlanta, GA 30324

Binks Mfg. Co.
9201 W. Belmont Ave.
Franklin Park, IL 60131

Blast-It-All, Inc.
Circle M, Industrial Park
Highway 29, So., P.O. Box 1615
Salisbury, NC 28144

W. H. Brady Co.
2223 W. Camden Rd.
P.O. Box 2131
Milwaukee, WI 53201

Brookstone Co.
127 Vose Farm Rd.
Peterborough, NH 03458

Buck Bros., Inc.
Millbury, MA 01527

Buhl Inc.
5 Paul Kohner Pl.
Elmwood Park, NJ 07407

Buhl Optical
1009 Beach Ave.
Pittsburgh, PA 15233

Chartpak, Div. Avery Prod. Corp.
One River Road
Leeds, MA 01053

Chromatic Paint Corp.
P.O. Box 105
Garnerville, NY 10923

Classic Images, Inc.
5656 Opportunity Dr.
Toledo, OH 43612

Cleveland Metal Abrasive Co.
888 E. 67th St.
Cleveland, OH

Albert Constantine & Son, Inc.
2050 Eastchester Rd.
Bronx, NY 10461

Consumers Paint Factory
Gary, IN 46406

Craftsman Wood Service Co.
2727 So. Mary St.
Chicago, IL 60608

The Craftool Co.
1421 240th St.
Harbor City, CA 90710

CraftPlans
Rogers, MN 55374

Custom Coated Products
Div. Payco Corp.
1280 Glendale-Milford Rd.
Cincinnati, OH 45215

Danacolors, Inc.
1833 Egbert Ave.
P.O. Box 24212
San Francisco, CA 94124

Edward W. Daniel Co.
4049-4115 St. Clair Ave.
Cleveland, OH 44103

Demco Educational Corp.
P.O. Box 7488
Madison, WI 53707

Deluxe Saw & Tool Co.
121 S. Jackson St.
Louisville, KY 40202

Demolux, Inc.
1 Madison St.
East Rutherford, NJ 07073

Die-Kuts, Inc.
183 St. Paul St.
Rochester, NY 14604

Display Craft, Inc.
P.O. Box 1206
Portland, IN 47371

Dremel Mfg.
Div. Emerson Electric Co.
4915 — 21st St.
Racine, WI 53406

Ekstrom, Carlson & Co.
1400 Railroad Ave.
Rockford, IL 61110

Elmo Mfg. Corp.
70 New Hyde Park Rd.
New Hyde Park, NY 11040

Exolon Company
949 E. Niagara St.
Tonawanda, NY

Lany Fax of America Inc.
4820 W. 128th Pl.
Alsip, IL 60658

Frog Tool Co. Ltd.
700 W. Jackson Blvd.
Chicago, IL 60606

Garrett Wade Co., Inc.
161 Avenue of Americas
New York, NY 10013

General Scientific Equipment Co.
Limeklin Pike & Williams Ave.
Philadelphia, PA 19150

Geougeon Brothers, Inc.
706 Martin St.
Bay City, MI 48706

Graphic Products Corp.
Rolling Meadows, IL 60008

Griffin Mfg. Co., Inc.
1660 Ridge Rd. E.
Webster, NY 14580

Hallcraft Products Co.
Sumneytown, PA 18084

John Harra Wood & Supply Co.
511 West 25th St.
New York, NY 10001

Walter Hartlauer
5377 Bailey Hill Road
Eugene, OR 97405

Harwell's Enterprises
P.O. Box 96
Byrdstown, TN 38549

Hearlihy & Co.
714 W. Columbia St.
Springfield, OH 45501

Her-Saf Products
Atascadero, CA 93422

Hoppmann Corp.
P.O. Box 1463
5410 Port Royal Rd.
Springfield, VA 22151

Hunter Associates
792 Partridge Dr.
Bridgewater, NJ 08807

Industrial Safety & Security Co.
1550 Elida Rd.
Lima, OH 45805

Integrated Laser Systems, Inc.
346 Rancheros Dr.
San Marcos, CA 92069

Johnson Plastics
Div. Signcaster Corp.
P.O. Box 20456
Minneapolis, MN 55420

K C Graphics, Inc.
1101 Cambridge Circle Dr.
P.O. Box 2914
Kansas City, KS 66110

Kalart Victor Corp.
P.O. Box 112
Hultenius St.
Plainville, CT 06062

W. H. Kemp Div.
Absolute Coatings Inc.
34 Industrial St.
Bronx, NY 10461

Kimball Woodcarver Co.
2602 Whitaker St.
Savannah, GA 31401

Kinduell Screen Products, Inc.
110 Center St., Wilder
Newport, KY 41071

Kurt Manufacturing Co.
1720 Marshall St., N.E.
Minneapolis, MN 55413

Kurz-Hastings, Inc.
Dutton Road
Philadelphia, PA 19154

Laskowski Enterprises, Inc.
4004 W. 10th St.
Indianapolis, IN 46222

Leichtung Inc.
701 Beta Drive No. 17
Cleveland, OH 44143

Letraset USA, Inc.
40 Eisenhower Dr.
Paramus, NJ 07652

Letter-Rite, Inc.
8219 W. Irving Park Rd.
Chicago, IL 60634

P. K. Lindsay Co., Inc.
Deerfield, NH 03037

Lineberry Foundry & Mach. Co.
North Wilkesboro, NC 28659

Luminos Photo Corp.
25 Wolffe St.
Yonkers, NY 10019

Luxite Corp.
85 Liberty Ave.
Jersey City, NJ 07306

Manhattan Wood Letter Co.
145-151 West 18th St.
New York, NY 10011

Marlin Industries
Route 70, Box 191
Cashiers, NC 28717 1320

Mastercraft Plans
Box 631
Park Ridge, IL 60068

Miro-Beads Inc.
2505 Albion St.
Toledo, OH

Millers Falls Div.,
Ingersoll-Rand
Greenfield, MA 01301

Mutual Aids
1953½ Hillhurst Ave.
Los Angeles, CA 90027

North American Products Corp.
Box 291
Jasper, IN 47546

Northeast Power Products, Inc.
300 Green Wood Ave.
Midland Park, NJ 07432

Oakland Carbide Engineering
   & Mfg. Co.
1232 Fifth-One Ave.
Oakland, CA 94601

Onsrud Cutter Mfg. Co., Inc.
800 East Broadway
Libertyville, IL 60048

Ottawa Silica Co.
Box 577
Ottawa, IL 63150

Paulow Industries
535 N. 53rd St.
Milwaukee, WI 53208

George Pfaff, Inc.
Box 837
Amityville, NY 11701

Pressure Graphics, Inc.
4636 West Fulton St.
Chicago, IL 60644

Projection Optics Co., Inc.
8 Fernwood Rd.
Florham Park, NJ 07932

Quality Industries, Inc.
Hillsdale Industrial Park
P.O. Box 278
Hillsdale, MI 49242

Rigyt Damar
Div. Potts Optics & Mfg. Co.
6336 E. 13th St.
Tulsa, OK 74112

Rockwell Power Tools
400 N. Lexington Ave.
Pittsburgh, PA 15208

Ruemelin Mfg. Co.
3844 N. Palmer St.
Milwaukee, WI 53212

Cecil E. Sanders Co.
R.R. 1 Box 155
Greenfield, IN 46140

Sav-Sets Div.
Kinduell Screen Products, Inc.
110 Center St., Wilder
Newport, KY 41071

Charles G.G. Schmidt & Co.
Montvale, NJ 07645

Sears Roebuck & Co.
Industrial Products
7447 Skokie Blvd.
Dept. 4570
Skokie, IL 60077

School Products Co. Inc.
1201 Broadway
New York, NY 10001

George R. Snell Associates, Inc.
155 U.S. Route 22
Springfield, NJ 07081

Southern Sign Supply Inc.
129 Roesler Rd.
Glen Burne, MD 21061

Spielmans Wood Works
188 Gibraltar Rd.
Fish Creek, WI 54212

Squibb-Taylor, Inc.
P.O. Box 20158 Harry Hines Blvd.
Dallas, TX 75220

Standard Projector & Equip. Co., Inc.
1911 Pickwick Ave.
Glenview, IL 60025

Stanley Power Tools
New Bern, NC 28560

T.M. Visual Industries Inc.
25 W. 45th St.
New York, NY 10036

Testrite Instrument Co., Inc.
135 Monroe St.
Newark, NJ 07105

3-M Company
Branch Sales Office
(or write)
Household & Hardware
   Products Div.
3-M Center
St. Paul, MN 55101

3-M Company
Industrial Tape Division
3-M Company
St. Paul, MN 55101

3-M Visual Products Div.
3-M Center
Building 220-10W
St. Paul, MN 55101

Titan Abrasive Systems, Inc.
P.O. Box 3, 30 Rogers Rd.
Furlong, PA 18925

Triarco Arts & Crafts
14650 28th Ave., No.
Plymouth, MN 55441

Universal Adhesives
576 56th St.
West New York, NJ 07093

Universal Metal Chain Co., Inc.
2 Ackerman Ave.
Clifton, NJ 07011

The Upholstery Supply Co.
12530 W. Burleigh Rd.
Brookfield, WI 53005

Virginia Machine Tool Co.
Bassett, VA

Visionvue Instruments
P.O. Box 151
Drumright, OK 74030

Weird Wood Co.
Green Mountain Cabins
Box 190B
Chester VT 05143

Weiser — Robodyne Corp.
949 Bonifant St.
Silver Spring, MD 20910

Wensco Sign Supplies
Box 1728
Grand Rapids, MI 49501

Wisconsin Knife Works
Beloit, WI 53511

A. Van Wormer
1904 Junction
Kalamazoo, MI 49001

Wood Graphics Co.
82 Aero Camino
Goleta, CA 93017

Woodcarvers Supply Co.
3112 W. 28th St.
Minneapolis, MN 55416

Woodcraft Supply Corp.
313 Montvale Ave.
Woburn, MA 01888

The Woodworkers Store
21801 Industrial Boulevard
Rogers, MN 55374

Zipatone Inc.
150 Fencl Lane
Hillside, IL 60162

# Index